Viper
Buyer's Guide

Maurice Q. Liang

MOTORBOOKS
INTERNATIONAL

On the front cover: *(main)* 1996 GTS Coupe. *Ron Kimball (top right)* The heart of a Viper—its V-10 engine. *Ron Kimball (middle right)* The early Viper interior. *Maurice Q. Liang (bottom right)* The Viper RT/10s signature 3-spoke wheel. *Ron Kimball*

About the author:
Maurice Q. Liang has been a carnut all his life. Since he was a child, he has collected toy cars. As an adult, he's owned European sports cars, classic American muscle cars, and Japanese "rice-rockets." But it wasn't until 1989 that he finally discovered his dream car—the Dodge Viper RT/10 concept car—on the cover of *Road & Track* magazine. He was bitten. From that moment on, he has been a Viperholic.

Liang has over 10 years and 100,000 miles of Viper ownership experience as the original owner of a red 1993 RT/10 roadster and the first blue with white stripes 1996 GTS coupe built for an outside customer.

His passion for the Viper led him to start the Viper Club of America. With the help of Steve Ferguson, Jay Herbert, and other Viper enthusiasts, and the support of Chrysler execs Bob Lutz, Tom Gale, Francois Castaing, Mary Levine, and Ron Smith, Liang formed what is now one of the premier car-owner clubs in the world.

Edited by Heather Oakley and Peter Bodensteiner
Designed by Mandy Iverson

Printed in China

Contents

Dedication

In memory of Brian Angen, son of Viper Club of America members Terri and Rocky Angen. Brian was uncannily fast on the track—despite having lost the use of one eye in his youth. At 23, he was on his way to becoming a professional race car driver when he lost his life in a tragic boating accident.

In life, Brian inspired the potential in all who knew him. In his passing, Brian brought us closer together and showed us the meaning and importance of friendships.

Brian is gone, but not forgotten.

The Brian Angen Memorial Foundation was established to keep the memory of Brian Angen alive and help less fortunate children in need. Tax-deductible contributions are welcome and may be sent to:

The Brian Angen Memorial Foundation
P.O. Box 320111
Los Gatos, CA 95032

Foreword

I'm pleased to have been asked by the author to contribute the foreword to this literary monument to what can only be called a monumental car: the stunning, original Dodge Viper.

In 1986 and 1987, Chrysler Design, under Tom Gale, had been experimenting with a number of concepts for sports-cars of various sizes, including a hoped-for compact roadster dubbed Sling Shot, and a much larger V-8–powered Corvette competitor code-named Big Shot. While original in shape, Big Shot lacked emotional impact and was little more than a clay-model curiosity, since Chrysler, at the time, had neither the funding nor the rear-wheel-drive componentry to implement such a program. Worse, the car would have been a me-too of the Corvette, even at the time, was already in its fourth generation, was enormously well developed, and looked back on a long tradition of commercial and racing successes. In short, there was little enthusiasm for Big Shot.

Having "transferred" from Ford in 1986, I still had (in fact, still have) in my possession a 1985 MK IV Autokraft all-aluminum "continuation" Cobra, built on the original chassis and using a Jack Roush–modified 302 V-8 making 300-brake-horsepower driving through a Warner T5 transmission. With its low weight and Ford-assisted chassis development, it was, and is, a wonderfully rewarding car to drive.

Enjoying it one Sunday afternoon in 1988 (I was President of Chrysler at the time), I reflected on my feelings of guilt at enjoying a car that was symbolic of a competitor's heritage. (I had earlier removed the "Powered by Ford" badges from the flanks!) "What a shame," I thought, "that Chrysler has nothing like this. It would really help to add a little spice to the excellent but somewhat boring, ever-expanding portfolio of front-wheel-drive K cars."

It suddenly dawned on me that our future pickup plans contained at least some of the essential ingredients: we were planning a massive 8-liter, V-10 engine, a new five-speed manual transmission, and independent front suspension parts of suitable heft. What the components lacked in nobility was

Bob Lutz with his other fast toys, his helicopter and jet.

compensated by their potential easy availability. By using proto-type parts, we could do a "one-off!"

I mentioned my dream to Francois Castaing, our newly appointed head of Engineering, and to Tom Gale, and the sur-reptitious skunk-works scheming began at once. Neither of them needed convincing!

As is now well documented, I did not like the early sketches, having mentally pictured something more akin to an updated Cobra with a longer hood, but I curbed my urge to intervene. Experience has taught me, as in the case of the later Cadillac "Art and Science" design theme, that designs that scare me initially may just, in fact, be so advanced and ground-breaking that they require an adjustment period. In any case, Francois and Tom prevailed, and I'm glad they did!

All my doubts were erased when I saw the first clay model, with its powerful, bulging surfaces and its heroic proportions. We all knew we had to have it as a concept car for the '89 Detroit Auto Show!

The rest, of course, is history, carefully documented here by the incredible Maurice Q. Liang, surely the most severely snake-bitten

"Viperholic" of all time. For every exotic car, there is a group of specialists, with an enthusiasm and a profound knowledge of their subject matter that is truly encyclopedic. But none I have met can match Maurice. As the 1992 Viper entered production, he made it his life mission to collect every auto show "saver"—every brochure, every poster, every model of every scale, every Viper napkin, ballpoint, notepad, video—everything and anything that pertained to the car of his dreams. And, of course, he became one of the earliest owners, as well as the founder of the first Viper owners' club. His home, once a comfortable and reasonably traditional dwelling was transformed into an international Viper shrine. I suspect it was a causal factor in the unfortunate demise of his marriage, for even the most patient of wives must surely resent having her carefully decorated home transformed into a cross between a museum and a toy store, all devoted to one car in one color!

So, like all true artists, Maurice suffered for his passion. His sacrifices, however, are our gain, for he has crafted the ultimate work on Viper, the complete history—the big story as well as the seemingly trivial esoterica.

Of devotion such as his are great works born. This book is a fitting tribute to a much-loved car: the beast that stunned the world, the car that transformed the tarnished image of Dodge and, with it, the entire Chrysler Corporation.

Despite my current position as Chairman of General Motors North America and my responsibility to the outstanding new C6 Corvette, the Viper's natural enemy (although they coexist nicely, and many enthusiasts own one or more of each), I am proud of the role I was permitted to play in the creation of an American icon.

I know I speak for many when I express my deep appreciation to Maurice for having chronicled Viper's history with such devotion to truth and accuracy.

There will never be a better Viper book!

Robert A. Lutz
Vice Chairman
Product Development
Chairman
General Motors North America

Introduction

As I write this book, I'm amused by an ad I see for a used Viper GTS claiming, "1 of only 500 pace cars made in blue with white stripes." Say what? I was already deeply immersed in Vipers when the coupe was launched, so I know that Dodge built 1,166 blue with white stripe GTSs in 1996. I also know that none came from the factory with Indy Pace Car decals—the decals were sold separately, and only 100 sets were made.

So, is this person trying to pull the wool over someone's eyes or simply misguided? It's my hope that this *Viper Buyer's Guide* will clarify some of these myths and be an easy-to-use reference guide for prospective Viper owners.

This guide lists the differences between models and years to help you choose which is best for you. It'll also give you tips on where to shop and what to look for, and it'll give you a taste of what it's like to own and drive a Viper as told by owners and magazine test reports. When you're done reading this guide, I hope you'll be started on the right foot of your Viper experience.

In researching and writing this guide, I've found myself crossing over from "Viperholic" to "Viper-Geek." Before, I was simply a rabid fan of the Viper. Now, my brain is filled with minute details like the roof-pin length on a 1992 RT/10—12 mm instead of the 18, 20, or 22 mm used on the 1993–1994. Fortunately, age will probably erase all this from my memory banks, but at least now it's documented!

Despite an author's most diligent efforts, no book is beyond correction. Mistakes surface. New information comes to light. To make this book more interactive, I have created a website—www.viperbuyersguide.com—where I will post any corrections and updates. You'll also find other resources to help you in your quest to become a Viper owner. While I have endeavored to be accurate, no doubt I've missed something. If you have any documented corrections or additions, or comments and suggestions, please contact me through this website.

I must thank a number of people for their help, including Dan Knott, Jeff Donaldson, Charlie Brown, and the rest of the staff at DaimlerChrysler's SRT Operations; Jon Brobst (Mr. Viper parts), Jay Herbert (International Viper Registry) for contributing to my research, and Randy Davis for reviewing my draft manuscript. My thanks to longtime friend and Viper tech, Ted May of Valaya Racing, who shared his experience and knowledge of the common problems he's found through servicing and modifying Vipers.

Many of the beautiful images you see in this book are the work of my friend and world-renowned car photographer, Ron Kimball. My thanks to him for contributing his work to this book giving it an even classier touch.

Of course, we should all thank Bob Lutz. For without his vision and cojones, the Viper would never have existed in the first place, and I, for one, would have a very different life. I also have to thank his lovely wife, Denise, who gave up her seat for the inaugural ride of the Viper GTS/R around Laguna Seca, so that this Viperholic could have a very unique experience—to my knowledge, it was the *only* time the GTS/R had a passenger seat.

Of course, it also took the dedication and hard work of the men and women of Team Viper to design, engineer, build, and market the Viper as well. In addition, we should thank the new management at DaimlerChrysler who "get" the Viper, which will ensure that the legend will live on.

I thank all my friends in the Viper Club of America. Many of them took the time to contribute their Viper stories to help you, the prospective Viper owner, know in your heart that this will be the right experience for you. In addition, they have contributed so much to my life story as well.

My heartfelt thanks to Peter Bodensteiner, and the good people at MBI Publishing Company who were willing to take the chance and publish this book and agreed to have me author it.

On a personal note, I must say a word of thanks to my parents, who insisted that I get a good education. They also indulged my interests in cars and photography from a young age. Because of their support and encouragement, I was able to participate in this exciting chapter of automotive history and now author this book.

I pass along that advice to any of you younger readers who dream about the day you'll own a Viper. Get a good education, work hard, and buy that bitchin' car! Meanwhile, thanks for buying this book!

Drive fast, take chances,
—Maurice Q. Liang
Los Altos, CA

1996 GTS flanked by a red '98 RT/10 and a '98 GT2. *Maurice Q. Liang*

Chapter 1

Introduction to Vipers

So, you've finally decided it's time to make good on that promise to buy yourself a Viper. The next question is usually, "Which one should I get?" From a distance, all Vipers may seem similar. But up close, you'll find that numerous changes and improvements have been made throughout the three generations of production. With some cars like Porsches, the general rule is "buy the newest one you can afford." But that's not necessarily true with Vipers.

Some people prefer the latest version with its increased horsepower and higher level of refinement while others prefer the rawness of the "classic" sidepipe Viper, with its no frills, no door handles, no windows, and a marginal roof. There is no one answer to the question, "Which is the best Viper?" It's a matter of personal preference.

IS A VIPER RIGHT FOR YOU?

Perhaps it's best to say this up front. The Viper is not for everyone. Do you want a car with all the toys like ABS, traction control, GPS, and power everything? Do you value a high level of refinement and luxurious materials? Do you prefer a smooth, quiet, comfortable ride? Do you want an automatic transmission? Do you like to be stealthy? If you answer yes to any of these questions, you may want to consider another car—because you probably won't be happy with a Viper.

With a Viper, you have to put up with some inconveniences: a front spoiler that scrapes easily, no side windows (on earlier cars, at least), bumping your head on the roof as you get in and out, burning your leg on the hot side sills, air conditioning that has no temperature adjustment, etc. But fortunately, unlike many exotics, it's a relatively low-maintenance car and doesn't demand $5,000+ tune-ups.

The Viper is about pure performance. It's rude, crude, and unrefined—and makes no apologies about it. It truly is the ultimate driving machine for those who can appreciate it. And it rewards you with amusement park–like thrills.

As I've often said, the Viper is more than a car—it's an experience. From the little tingle you get whenever you see that curvaceous body sitting in your garage, to the thrill you get every time you stomp on the loud pedal, to the wonderful people you meet just because it's a conversation starter, it's truly an incredible experience.

A BRIEF HISTORY

It began one afternoon in 1988 with a glint in Bob Lutz's eye, when he was out driving his Autokraft Cobra. "Why can't we build a modern-day Cobra from the parts we have, the way we *remember* the original Cobra to be?" he thought. While many of us may have thoughts like that, Lutz had a much bigger parts bin to choose from—he was President of Chrysler. "Why not take the new V-10 engine being developed for the Ram pickup and drop it into a back-to-basics roadster?" he thought. It would be the perfect image car Chrysler needed to signify their turnaround.

After some discussion with Tom Gale, then Vice President of Design at Chrysler, and Francois Castaing, then VP of Engineering for Chrysler, sketches were developed and eventually a concept car was built by Metalcrafters for the 1989 North American International Auto Show in Detroit.

The Viper was a hit. The promise of good old American muscle with European sports car handling wrapped in voluptuous body struck a nerve with thousands of car enthusiasts who had been numbed by the dullness of the late '70s and early '80s emissions-control-laden, landau-roofed, wire-hubcapped cars. Enthusiasts who missed out on owning a Cobra in the '60s saw the Viper as their second chance. Letters and checks poured in.

Several books have been written documenting the development of the car, so I'll spare you the details here. Suffice it to say that a small team was pulled together, led by Executive Engineer Roy Sjoberg, to evaluate, engineer, and eventually build the stunning roadster. Lamborghini, then owned by Chrysler, helped the team turn the cast-iron block truck engine into an aluminum block performance car engine.

Bob Lutz, then-President of Chrysler, is considered the father of the Viper.

The Viper RT/10 concept car drew rave reviews at the 1989 Detroit Auto Show.

Bob Lutz and Team Viper unveiled the production-ready Viper RT/10 at the 1992 auto show in Detroit. Normally jaded journalists applauded.

Dealer markup was rampant in the first year as dealers scrambled to capitalize on the first limited-production American exotic car. This dealer added $199,999 to the sticker price.

The car was so popular that even before any were produced for sale, the Viper was drafted at pace car duty for the 1991 Indy 500. A prototype was used, and engineers took advantage of the track time to test the car. Carroll Shelby, father of the Cobra, was pulled in as a spiritual consultant to Team Viper and served as the pace car driver.

On a cold Detroit morning in January of 1992, an enormous crowd of journalists from around the world gathered at the North American International Auto Show to witness Lutz, Shelby, and Team Viper unveil their production-ready baby to the public.

The year 1992 marked the first production of the Viper RT/10. Only 285 cars were made that year, hardly enough to satisfy the pent-up demand. Dealer-markup was rampant—some as high as $199,999!

Over the next 10 years, more than 15,000 Vipers were built, with many refinements and improvements made along the way. Officially, there are three generations of Vipers now: the 1992–1995 RT/10 roadster, the 1996–2002 RT/10 roadster and GTS coupe, and the 2003+ SRT-10 convertible.

OVERVIEW OF THREE GENERATIONS

Gen I: The "Classic" RT/10 Roadster

In Viper-speak, the original Viper RT/10 (which stood for Road and Track, 10 cylinder) is often referred to as the roadster. By classic definition, a roadster has no top or side windows. And that's how the original Viper was envisioned. But at the last minute, plastic clip-in side curtains and a basic folding canvas top were added to protect owners from unanticipated rainstorms.

The Viper's no-frills mission was and is, "If it doesn't make it go faster, it doesn't belong on the car." Consequently, there are few amenities. What it does have is a huge 8.0-liter 488-ci V-10 engine with 400 horsepower and, perhaps more importantly, 465 lb-ft[1] of torque for gut-wrenching acceleration. With its fully independent suspension and steamroller-sized tires, it handles as well as it accelerates. The side-piped "classic" version was produced from 1992 through 1995.

Gen II: The GTS coupe joins the roadster

At the 1993 Los Angeles Auto Show, Dodge teased the public with a concept coupe version of the Viper. It had a fixed double-bubble hardtop, glass hatchback, and ducktail spoiler. Painted a deep metallic blue with dual white stripes, it was patterned after the

The first-generation, side-piped "classic" Viper, produced from 1992 through 1995 was a true roadster with no roll-up windows, no outside door handles, and a minimal roof (shown with later-style five-spoke wheels). Owner: Maurice Q. Liang.

Dodge captured lightning in a bottle a second time with the coupe version of the Viper, known as the GTS, patterned after the Shelby Daytona Coupes of the 1960s.

[1] Over the years, Dodge's documentation has rated the original Viper V-10's peak torque at 450 lb-ft, 465 lb-ft, and 480 lb-ft.

In 1999, Dodge introduced the ACR (American Club Racer) option on GTSs for Viper enthusiasts who wanted to go racing on the weekends. Owner: Fred Kinder.

Shelby Daytona coupe from the 1960s. Chrysler captured lightning in a bottle a second time as the public (many of them already Viper RT/10 owners) urged Chrysler to put the coupe into production.

In 1996, the second generation of Vipers began with the introduction of the production Viper GTS (Grand Touring Sport) coupe. Not just a roadster with a coupe body, the GTS featured a re-designed chassis, a re-designed V-10 engine—now with 450 horsepower and 490 lb-ft of torque, rear-exit exhaust, and "luxury" amenities like outside door handles and roll-up side windows.

Since the 1996 roadsters were produced before the coupes, they were somewhat of a transitional car, retaining the old-style body, interior, and engine (now with 415 horsepower), but receiving the coupe's all-new chassis, suspension, five-spoke wheels, rear-exit exhaust, and new Michelin Pilot SX tires for improved wet weather traction.

In 1997 the RT/10 received more updates including a new interior, engine, roll-up windows, and outside door handles. But it wasn't until 1998 that the roadster featured the coupe's hood with its NACA duct (National Advisory Committee for Aeronautics duct) and vents. Further improvements and refinements were made to the second-generation Vipers through 2002.

In addition, a pure race version was built; it was called the GTS/R. A limited-edition replica of the GTS/R, referred to as the "GT2," was built for the street in 1998. For weekend racers, Dodge added the ACR (American Club Racing) performance option to GTSs in 1999.

GEN III: The SRT-10

Though still able to draw a crowd, the Viper was 10 years old in 2002, so Dodge's halo car was given a complete re-design for 2003. The third-generation Viper SRT-10 (Street and Racing Technology, 10 cylinder) is a true convertible, with a soft top that manually folds into the trunk. The SRT-10 features an all-new chassis with a slightly longer wheelbase, an all-new race-inspired interior,

The 1996 RT/10 roadsters were a transitional car, consisting mostly of the older roadster but with the GTS's new chassis, wheels, and rear-exit exhaust. Three unique color schemes were created for this year. *Chrysler*

Second-generation RT/10s received the GTS's updated chassis, 450-horsepower engine, roll-up windows, outside door handles, new front fascia, and vented hood with NACA duct. Owner: Brett Pearson.

The third generation of Vipers began in 2003 with the new SRT-10, a full convertible with 500 horsepower.

and an 8.3-liter 505-ci engine, now with 500 horsepower and 525 lb-ft of torque, still coupled to a six-speed manual transmission. Back are the side-exit exhausts and trademark Dodge cross-hair grill, but gone are the familiar Viper design cues of the rear sport bar, the rounded side vents, the "speaker-grill" air vents in the hood, and the forward-tilting clamshell hood.

Also built off the same (but highly modified) chassis is the Competition Coupe, a limited-production, track-only race car.

DECISIONS, DECISIONS. HOW DO YOU CHOOSE?

While it would be easy to divide this book into chapters covering the changes year-by-year, most Viper buyers don't shop that way. Before they are concerned about model year differences, they have first chosen a body style, color, and price range. Here are some factors to help you narrow your choices.

BODY STYLE

Choosing between a roadster, coupe, or convertible is mostly based upon how you plan to use your Viper and which look you prefer.

Do you plan to use your Viper on a daily basis in all kinds of weather? Do you frequently park in the city where you need to lock your car? Does the temperature vary a lot where you live? Do you plan to use your Viper on the track? Is wind-mussed hair going to be a problem for you or your spouse? If so, then you may prefer the fixed roof and roll-up windows of the GTS coupe.

However, there's nothing like an RT/10 if you crave that wind-in-your-face experience. Make that a tornado-in-your-face experience. Adding a hardtop to an RT/10 allows you to have the wind-in-your-face plus the comfort and security of a coupe. The only drawback is, when you store the soft top (and side curtains) in the trunk, you lose half of the already-limited luggage space.

The beauty of the new Viper SRT-10 convertible is that you can decide on the spot whether you want open or closed motoring—without having to sacrifice any trunk space.

Other factors to consider: Do you want to be able to take a child in a child seat for a ride with you? If so, you'll need to avoid 1996–1997 GTSs and 1997 RT/10s because they have air bags, but no cut off switches.

Are you short? Many drivers under 5' 7" have trouble reaching the pedals on the early cars. If you're vertically-challenged, you may want to consider the Gen II and III cars with their adjustable pedal clusters.

Are you tall? Many drivers over 6' 2" have trouble fitting in Gen I and II Vipers. It's best to test fit yourself first. Some tall drivers lower the driver's seat to fit.

Styling, of course, is subjective. Some Viper owners feel very strongly about the styling of the different models—enough that they won't even consider another choice. For many, it has to be the low, squat look of the original side-pipe classic roadster. Others consider the lines of the coupe, with its double-bubble roof and ducktail spoiler to be the ultimate. And still others prefer the more "refined" look of the new SRT-10.

Having trouble deciding? Then join the 25 percent or so owners who don't decide and just buy more than one Viper!

COLOR

When you think about your dream Viper, is it a specific color? If your heart is set on a particular color combination, this may limit you to specific model years. For many, it's red for the RT/10, or blue with white stripes for a GTS.

Red is easy. Since that's Dodge's corporate color, red has been available on every year and model Viper except for the 1996 GTS coupe. A blue with white stripes coupe is more limiting, since that color combination was only available in 1996 and 1997. A blue with white stripes RT/10 is even tougher. Only 53 of these were built in 1997. If sinister black is your color, then it has to be 1993 through 1995, 1999, and 2000 for an RT/10, or 1999 and 2000 for a GTS. For a quick summary of color choices, refer to the quick-reference guide in the back of this book.

PRICE

After the initial release, most cars depreciate in value. While Vipers may depreciate more slowly than the average car, they do nonetheless depreciate. Historically, most cars tend to reach their lowest value when they're around 10 to 15 years old. After that, if they're collectible, they begin to appreciate in value.

This is good news for those of you who have held off buying a Viper because you're price-challenged. At the time this book is first being printed, the oldest Vipers are around 10 years old, so prices are reaching their lowest point. Now is a great time to pick up a first-generation Viper roadster. It's likely that Vipers (in good condition) will never drop much below $30,000 because there are far more people willing to pay that amount for a Viper than there are Vipers available. It's the basic law of supply and demand.

The Competition Coupe is a limited-production, track-only coupe version of the new Viper built for serious racers. Owners: Frank Parise, Bob Woodhouse, and Dennis McCann. *Maurice Q. Liang*

So, if finding the lowest price is your main concern, there's no point in considering a GTS or an SRT-10. The 1992–1995 roadsters are the lowest-priced Vipers, since they are the oldest.

When shopping for a Viper, there are some things to look for that are common to all Vipers, regardless of year, model, or color. These are covered in the following chapter. After that, each chapter covers a different category of Viper (e.g., roadsters, coupes, and convertibles) and the changes for each model year.

COLLECTIBILITY RATINGS

The star ratings used in this book are relative to Vipers only, not to other cars.

***** = The most collectible, desirable Vipers

**** = Likely to be a desirable Viper

*** = Above average in collectibility

** = Average

* = Avoid (No Vipers are in this category.)

This Viper sits in a used car lot, waiting for a new owner.

Chapter 2

Shopping for a Viper

BUYING NEW VIPERS

If you want to be the original owner of a new Viper, then your only choice is a Dodge dealer. Technically, Vipers are built on a "Sold Order" basis, meaning they shouldn't be ordered until there is a customer who has already committed to it. However, many dealers still order Vipers so they can have Vipers on display and in stock for immediate delivery.

While any Dodge dealer can order a Viper, it's generally best to find a dealer that specializes in selling (and servicing) Vipers. You're more likely to get knowledgeable sales people and reasonable prices from these dealers. Call ahead to determine who at the dealership is responsible for selling Vipers *before* you walk in. It's often the Fleet Manager or the Sales Manager. This way, you can avoid the uninformed "middle-man." You can usually find dealers who specialize in Vipers by checking with your closest Viper club president or by going online and visiting the official Viper Club of America website at www.viperclub.org or checking the book's website at www.viperbuyersguide.com.

If you're placing an order, remember, dealers are independent businesses, so until you have a Vehicle Order Number (VON) assigned by DaimlerChrysler Corporation, all you have is an agreement with your friendly Dodge dealer. During the early days when Vipers were in short supply, many customers thought they had a "confirmed" order for a Viper by giving their dealer a deposit, but in actuality, Chrysler had not yet taken orders or scheduled any cars for production.

Yes, you can buy a "new" as in never-driven Viper from a broker, but generally, you are not considered the original registered owner as far as the manufacturer is concerned. Is this important? That depends upon how important the ramifications are to you.

First, there's the warranty period. While the factory warranty is transferable, the clock starts ticking when the vehicle is put "in-service,"—the date the car was first delivered from the dealer. If the broker has sat on the car for months, then the warranty period is that much shorter for you.

A second consideration is whether you'll want to participate in any customer loyalty reward programs Dodge may offer. For example, when the GTS coupe and the SRT-10 convertible were introduced, Dodge rewarded *original* Viper owners with a coupon that enabled them to receive priority scheduling for the first year of production. Without this coupon, dealers couldn't order a first-year car. This helped loyal Viper owners avoid price gouging and gave them first shot at owning the new cars. To qualify for the coupon, you had to be the original registered owner and still own your Viper. Those who bought their Vipers through brokers or secondhand did not qualify.

It's customary to test drive a car before you purchase it. But as you can imagine, Dodge dealers are flooded with requests to "test drive" a Viper, with the buyer having no serious intention of purchasing the car. Add to that the horror stories of people wrecking Vipers on their first trip around the block because they're not used to all that torque and it's no wonder dealers are reluctant to let you test drive a new Viper. Besides, think about it, if you were to be the owner of this "new" Viper, would you want a bunch of people taking joy rides in it first? Consequently, you'll often find it difficult to test drive a Viper at a dealer, even if they have one in stock.

At best, most dealers will say, "You purchase the car. If you don't like it, I'll give you your money back." If you really want to see what a Viper is like, seek out your local Viper club, and if you're nice about it, more than likely, they'd be happy to show you the car and possibly give you a ride.

The Viper comes with a standard three year/36,000 mile warranty. It covers any owner within that time/mileage. For most cars, I don't recommend an extended warranty, but for the Viper, it's worth it. One repair, like replacing a corroded Gen II side sill ($4,300 for the part plus paint and labor) will pay for the warranty. To save some money when purchasing your extended warranty, you can tailor the time and mileage limits to suit your use (e.g., low mileage and long time period). Note that Chrysler's extended warranty can only be transferred once. Aftermarket warranties (i.e., not Chrysler's) can be a risk, depending on the company that's selling them. Many have gone out of business, leaving the owner with no coverage. Also, be sure to read the fine print on what's covered and what's not.

BUYING PRE-OWNED VIPERS

Like any specialty car, you'll find Vipers listed in publications like the *Dupont Registry, Hemmings, AutoWeek*, and of course, on the Internet. The Viper Club of America's website (www.viper-club.org) also features one of the most visited classified sections for Vipers. If you live in a major metropolitan area, you may be able to find a car closer to home by looking in your local news-paper classifieds and in auto trader–publications.

Dodge dealers, auto brokers, and consignment stores also tend to carry pre-owned Vipers. It's always better if you can find one that specializes in Vipers, as they tend to sort the good ones from the bad ones.

Auctions can be tricky, as usually you have very limited access to the car and owner to determine the history of the car. What might seem like a good deal could turn out to be a night-mare when you get your low-mileage Viper home and find out it was a previous exotic car rental unit and has been wrecked and carelessly repaired several times.

As with any used car, the more you know about its history and its previous owner, the better your decision will be. Here again, it's wise to check with your closest Viper club. The Viper community is a small community, so in many cases, they may know the owner and the history of a given car, or they may know of a car that's available but not yet advertised. Generally, I've found that club members' cars are in above-average condition, as members tend to be the enthusiasts.

HOW VIPERS ARE BUILT

Understanding how a Viper is built will help you understand what to look for when shopping for a Viper.

Although Vipers go down an assembly line, they are still mostly put together by hand. There are no robots on the line. The chassis is assembled on the first half of the line. At one end, the bare frame goes in.

At the other end, the suspension, instrument panel, engine, wheels, and tires have been added to form a go-kart-like "hot chassis." This hot chassis, with no body panels attached yet, is run up through all gears to 80 miles per hour on the roller dyno.

Each body panel is hand finished at ASC.

Body panels arrive at the factory pre-painted.

The second half of the assembly line is where the body panels, glass, interior, and trim are installed. First- and second-generation Vipers are designed to be built from the center out—imagine laying a carpet by starting in the middle of the room and rolling the bumps out to the outside edges. Consequently, the tolerances can build up as the car is assembled. Shims are used to adjust for differ-ences in body panel fit. By the end of the line, it was often a challenge to line up the front fascia with the hood and head-lights. This explains why you'll find some Vipers with barely a gap between the hood and the top of the headlights, and others with a gap so big you can slide you hand through it.

A fully functional "hot chassis" is built up and tested on a dyno before body panels are installed.

After testing, body panels, interior, and trim are installed on this SRT-10.

The final piece to go on is the front fascia.

Unlike most vehicles at auto plants, Vipers are stored inside until ready for shipment in enclosed transporters.

SRT-10's are built with a new process called net, form, and pierce. A machine aligns the frame so all mounting points are precisely located, eliminating the need for shims.

Unlike unibody cars, where the entire body is painted at one time, Viper body panels arrive at the plant pre-painted. Panels on early cars were painted by different suppliers, making it a challenge to match paint. Later, one supplier (ASC, Inc. of Southgate, MI) took over painting all the panels, solving the problem.

All panels are hand-painted, sanded, and polished before being sent to the Viper assembly plant.

Since the panels were pre-painted, you might assume that any signs of overspray must indicate accident repair. However, this may not be true on 1996 and earlier Vipers. At the end of the line, all Vipers were quality inspected. If a flaw was found, it was sent to the rework area. If necessary, a part of the car was repainted. For example, I know my 1993 RT/10 has never been in an accident, because I've "known it" since it came off the delivery truck, yet there is a bit of overspray in the corner where the trunk lid meets the fender. On newer Vipers, if a flaw was found, the panels were replaced instead.

Likewise, if you find hairline cracks in the paint on the hood, you might assume the hood had been repaired from accident damage. This is not necessarily the case. The resin transfer molded (RTM) hood used on the 1992–1995 RT/10 was one of the largest pieces ever made using this process. As the part cured, the shrinkage rate was inconsistent. Most hoods required filling with Bondo and sanding by hand to achieve a smooth finish before painting. As the cars have aged, it's not unusual for the Bondo layer to shrink, causing hairline fractures in the paint. These can't be buffed out. If it has imperfections, decide if you can live with it. Refinishing a hood is an expensive proposition.

Original style replacement hoods are no longer available. The Gen I RTM hoods have been superseded by the later sheet molded compound (SMC) hood and cost around $17,000. While of better quality, these hoods are made from a different material, have the indents marked on the underside for the NACA duct and vents of the later-style cars, and often have more rounded corners near the headlight openings than the original hoods. So, if you're after a concours-correct Gen I Viper, even a factory replacement hood won't be correct—you'll have to track down a used hood.

WHAT TO LOOK FOR

It's important to understand what you want in your Viper. If you're looking for the cheapest Viper you can find, you don't care about condition, and you just plan to drive it into the ground, then most of what this guide covers is irrelevant.

However, if you want a car that is mostly original for show or maximum future resale value or if you plan to re-build a wreck to like-new condition, then it's important to pay attention to the details. Replacing damaged or missing original parts can be expensive! Many of the replacement parts for Vipers are no longer available through DaimlerChrysler. The limited-production nature of the car means it's unlikely aftermarket companies will reproduce many of the parts, or if they do, they'll charge a lot to recoup the tooling investment for such a low volume. Accordingly, if you need a replacement part, you'll have to find a used part in good condition (a challenge on its own), which may be quite expensive.

Consequently, it's best to buy a car that has most or all of the original parts. Factor in the cost, including labor, of replacing any worn or damaged part before grabbing that "great deal" that needs "minor" repair.

Before you purchase a used Viper, it's best to have an experienced Viper tech inspect it. Experienced techs know what to look for, what is right, and what is not correct. The information in this guide will help you do the preliminary inspection yourself.

OUTSIDE INSPECTION

Overall, is it a clean, like-new car or is it showing signs of wear?

The overspray on the driveshaft indicates this car has been (carelessly) repainted.

Look for scrapes on the bottom of front spoiler. If the spoiler is damaged, the entire front fascia must be replaced.

How is the paint? Is it peeling? Are the stripes lifting? If so, the car was probably left in the sun a lot.

Look carefully at the hood, particularly near the "speaker grill" vents. Do you see any hairline cracks from the factory Bondo curing? Are there bubbles in the paint? Some orange peel is normal in factory paint, but it should be shiny and deep. Are there signs of overspray where there shouldn't be? Look under the car. Overspray tends to collect on underside components like the driveshaft.

Look under the front spoiler. This is the most vulnerable part of the car. If the owner was careful, the spoiler may only have some minor scrapes or scratches. Contrary to what appears to be two pieces, the front spoiler and the fascia are one piece. If you have to replace the spoiler, the entire front fascia must be

Note the large gap between the hood and headlights. This does not necessarily indicate accident-damage repair. Build quality was inconsistent on earlier cars.

A seemingly minor item like these grommets for the side curtains can be expensive to replace ($48 each!). Factor these costs in if you plan to restore the car to like-new condition.

replaced. Original-style 1992–1997 fascias are no longer available, and the newer style fascia lists for $1,675.

If the fascia has been repainted while on the car, overspray may be on the black radiator or radiator support.

Look at the panel gaps, especially where the hood, headlight, and fascia come together. Are they even?

If a Viper has had the front fascia replaced, it can be difficult to get a replacement panel to fit like the original one. Look at the sharp corners of the hood. Are there any chips near the headlights or door edge? Those are often the places that are easily damaged in accidents. Look down the doors. Are there any chips? Vipers don't get door dings—they chip. Look near the trunk lock. Has it been scratched by the careless use of keys?

If it's a "classic" Viper with side curtains, look at the grommets where the side curtains plug in. Are they in good condition? Replacement grommets costs $48 *each*.

Check the triangular "bump" at the leading edge of the door. Many owners used this to pull the door closed, which causes the interior bezel to separate from the door panel and sometimes breaks the plastic tabs off the bezel. Replacement bezels are around $40.

Look along the sport bar. Is the paint scratched from misplacement of the roof latches? If it's a pre-1997 RT/10 and has the hardtop on it, does the owner have the black pad for the sport bar? The pad must be removed to install the hardtop, and if misplaced, they're difficult to obtain and cost over $1,000.

Check for cracks and chips in the windshield. Replacing a Viper windshield is around a $600 procedure. Are any of the emblems or badges missing? Typically, a replacement emblem costs $60.

It's not uncommon for side sills and covers to turn yellow from the exhaust heat.

Look around the cover plate between the front of the door and the back of the hood, above the side sill covers. It's not uncommon for this area to turn yellow due to excessive heat from the exhaust. It doesn't mean there's anything wrong or that the car has been abused, but depending upon your pickiness, it may require repainting all those parts.

Check the side sills, top and bottom. Are they dented or scraped? Replacement sills can cost $4,300 each plus painting.

Look at the front brake calipers. Is the lettering of "Viper" or "RT/10" still white? If it's yellow, it's likely due to hard braking during track use. (Not that there's anything wrong with it, but if you're looking for showroom new, this may be important to you.)

This dash panel has been painted red by the owner. New replacements are now difficult to obtain.

Look for worn leather parts like the shift knob, steering wheel, and emergency brake boot. A replacement steering wheel is over $800.

Yellowish tint on the caliper logo indicates brakes have seen high heat, probably from track use.

If it's an RT/10, check the condition of the folding soft top, the tonneau cover, and, if it's a pre-1997, the side curtains. If the soft top wasn't properly latched, it could have flown off and been damaged in the process. The plastic side curtains can become scratched and yellow with age. Is there a matching hard-top for the car? (They weren't standard equipment.)

Check the wheels, especially the right rear wheel. Typically it's prone to scrapes when parallel parking. On 1992–1995 RT/10s, the unidirectional three-spoke right rear wheels are harder to find because these are damaged the most.

INSIDE INSPECTION

Now let's turn our attention to the inside of the car. Is the dash panel in good condition? Depending on the year and model, replacement dash panels are difficult or impossible to obtain.

Look for wear on the leather shift knob, leather shift boot, e-brake boot, leather steering wheel, and pedal pads. These items wear easily and are costly to replace. Lift up on the shifter and

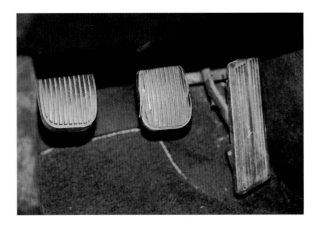

Worn pedal pads indicate use and likely higher mileage.

The side bolsters often wear out.

The holes in the rear bulkhead cover indicate five-point harnesses were installed. Possibly an indicator that the car was used on the track. If you want to restore the car to original condition, the cover will need to be replaced.

Carpet on lower part of door is often balled up.

Corrosion on the exposed metal bolt heads indicates this car was used in a wet (probably salty) climate.

make sure it's tight. If it moves, it's likely the rubber isolation mount has separated, which requires replacing the shifter.

Inspect the seats. Is the leather in good condition? Has the foam been crushed?

Look behind the seats. Unless the car is an ACR or GT2 that came with five-point harnesses, there shouldn't be any cutouts for seatbelts. If there are, was the car used on the track a lot? If you want to restore it to original condition, you'll have to replace the rear bulkhead cover, an expensive item.

Have the speaker areas been modified for aftermarket speakers? Many owners like to personalize their cars. If the

On this car, smooth intake tubes have replaced the stock corrugated tubes. While better for performance, be sure to get the original tubes if you want to be able to return the car to stock condition.

This heater air vent gasket often collapses over time.

stereo, shift knob, climate control knobs, and cigarette lighter are not original, does the owner have the original parts?

Look at the carpet along the bottom of the door. Is the pile even or is it balling up in fuzz? If possible, lift the front carpet along the edges and look for signs of water damage. Vipers are not the most waterproof cars ever built, and long periods of water standing under the carpets can cause rust or mold.

The re-welding and overspray on this frame indicate this car has had major accident repairs.

Look in the trunk. Is the compact spare still there? Are the tools there?

UNDER THE HOOD

Open the hood. Is the engine generally clean? Cars exposed to salt air will show corrosion around exposed metal parts.

Unless it's an ACR or GT2, the air filter housing should be a pair of black ribbed tubes. Many people replace these with "smooth tubes" and K&N air filters, which is fine. But if you want to be able to return it to stock, be sure to get the original housing.

Check the brake fluid. It should be fairly clear and not brown or black. Check the oil. It should be honey-colored. Check the power steering fluid. Look at the rubber donut gasket over the heater box. Is it in good shape? Most become squished over time. This part is available only as part of a gasket package, which costs over $100.

UNDER THE CAR

Put the car up on a hoist. (Or use jack stands, never just a jack!) Inspect the radiator support. If a car has had front-end damage, the radiator support is often damaged. Inspect the frames for welds where a subframe may have been grafted on to repair accident damage.

Also, look for signs of leaks, particularly on the lower part of the engine block. It's common for the head gasket to leak, leaving white stains on the block.

Is the exhaust original? Many owners replace the stock exhausts with aftermarket ones. Decide if having the original exhaust is important to you.

DOCUMENTATION

Good documentation is always a plus. For starters, the car should come with the owner's manual, which came in a leather pouch that also held the center-cap removal tool and warranty booklet. For 1992 cars, it should be a large valise.

Check to see if recall repairs have been done. Recall #979 required replacement of the five-point racing harnesses in 1998 GT2s and 1999–2001 ACRs. Recall #998 required repairs to the steering crossmember and differential mounting brackets on 1996–1999 Viper coupes and roadsters. Recall #999 reinforced the steering gear crossmember on 1999–2000 Viper coupes and roadsters. Ask if the owner has the service records and the original window sticker. If records are not available, DaimlerChrysler customer service can give you a printout of your vehicle's dealer service history.

TEST DRIVE

Now it's time to drive the car. The engine should fire up without much cranking. If it doesn't turn at all, make sure the clutch pedal is depressed all the way. Sometimes, the floor mat bunches up and prevents the clutch pedal from going all the way in.

The car should idle smoothly, though 1996–1999 GTSs and 1997–1999 RT/10s can be a bit "lopey" due to a more aggressive cam. If it's not idling smoothly, is missing, or seems down on power, check the spark plug wires. It's not uncommon for factory spark plug wires to crack and break due to the exhaust heat in less than 24,000 miles.

On coupes, you may hear a rattling sound when the car is in neutral with the clutch pedal out. It's known as "neutral gear rattle" and it's normal.

Check the clutch pressure. While it's difficult to tell unless you've just driven a new Viper, a Viper clutch gets heavier as it wears out. Eventually, the pressure needed to push the clutch in may bend the rod.

Be sure to do the basic functionality tests: lights, turn signals, horn, stereo, gauges, alarm system, air-conditioning (if so equipped), and so on.

Be careful with throttle application. The high amount of torque can spin the rear tires easily. On the other hand, if you accelerate too gingerly, the skip-shift device will force you to shift from first gear to fourth gear.

As you first drive off, listen for clunks and rattles. The U-joints on the axle half-shafts begin to wear on higher-mileage cars (more than 50,000 miles).

Shift up through the gears. There shouldn't be any grinding. If the shifter seems to hang when going into third gear, it may not actually be a problem. Drivers unfamiliar with the Viper often apply slight pressure to the right as they shift into third instead of pushing straight forward.

There shouldn't be any vibration through the steering wheel, though some hunting and dartiness are not unusual on rough and rutty surfaces, especially with first-generation roadsters riding on the original Michelin XGTZs. The tires are wide and tend to follow the imperfections in the road. If the hunting seems excessive, check the inside edges of the front tires for excessive wear. If the tires seem OK, a re-alignment to newer specifications may help.

On an empty road, with no cars behind you, test the brakes. Remember, only Vipers built from 2001 on have ABS, so be careful not to lock up the brakes and flat spot the tires.

Be careful pulling in and out of driveways. The front spoiler will scrape on relatively minor bumps. Always try to approach dips at a 45 degree angle so the tire contacts the rise before the nose of the car.

After driving the car, check under the hood and under the car for any leaks.

1993 RT/10 in front of Golden Gate Bridge. Owner: Maurice Q. Liang. *Ron Kimball*

Chapter 3

1992–2002
Viper RT/10 Roadsters

The "Classic" Roadster (1992–1995)

The first-generation "classic" roadster refers to the original-formula Viper—an open roadster with sidepipes, no roll-up windows, and a rudimentary soft top. All came with a 400-horsepower V-10, six-speed manual transmission, and three-spoke wheels. The highest production years for the Gen I Viper were 1994 and 1995, and these cars tended to have the best quality because most of the production bugs had been worked out.

Production of the roadsters began at the New Mack Assembly Plant in Detroit in early 1992. To make assembly easier, only one color combination was available that year—red with a gray leather interior. Since they were all the same color, if a particular panel didn't fit, another one could easily be substituted. Black was added in 1993, and Emerald Green and Dandelion Yellow were added for 1994 and 1995. No RT/10s came with stripes from the factory *except* for the partial stripes (from hood to trunk lid) on the 1996 RT/10 and the blue with white stripes 1997 RT/10.

In 1995, Dodge introduced a double-bubble hardtop that could be retrofitted to earlier cars. Although the roofs themselves were the same, different part numbers were necessary to distinguish the differences in the latch-pin designs over the years. For example, a 1992 top (soft or hard) will not latch on a 1993 car. There were even different pin lengths within model years, so if you are purchasing a replacement top, be sure you have the correct pins to fit your car.

Viper engines are designed to run hot, at 220°, so it's not uncommon for the temp gauge to hover near the caution zone. It *is* important to keep the coolant level topped off since a drop in coolant level can cause overheating. It's also important that air is bled out of the cooling system correctly to maintain cooling efficiency. This is particularly so on 1992–1993 Vipers, which are harder to bleed because they do not have the coolant overflow tanks.

Gas gauges on these cars are often inaccurate, and there is no fix for it. The gauge may reach the empty mark when as few as 16 of the 22 gallons of fuel have been used.

In terms of problems, most Gen I cars eventually develop a leak around the thermostat gasket because the thermostat housing straddles the two sides of the V of the back of the engine block. The different stresses on each side of the V cause the gasket to leak. Look for coolant in the valley under the intake manifold and sniff for coolant near the base of the windshield. The repair is not a big problem, but it will cost around $400.

Gen I engines use separate throttle cables for each of the throttle bodies, and occasionally, these cables need to be reset to maintain proper synchronization between the left and right throttle bodies to reduce jerking at low speeds.

If you like a wind-in-your-face, visceral experience, few cars compare with the classic RT/10 roadster.

1992 RT/10

Collectibility: ****

Only 285 Vipers were built in 1992, the first year of production at the New Mack Assembly Plant in Detroit. Two hundred cars were allocated to the U.S. market, the rest to international markets. Vehicle Identification Number (VIN) 1 through 17 were cars used for marketing, PR, engineering, and executives. Lee Iacocca, Chrysler's Chairman received VIN 1 and Bob Lutz, Chrysler's President, received VIN 2.

All cars were built in the same color combination to simplify ordering and production: Viper red (code PRN) with a quartz (gray) leather interior (code MLXD). The "classic" roadster featured an 8.0-liter 400-horsepower V-10, six-speed manual transmission (with no reverse lockout), side-exit exhausts, no outside door handles, and no roll-up windows. In 1992, the "toupee" roof was made of a stiff, pebble-grained vinyl.

The tires were considered extremely low profile at the time of the car's introduction, with Michelin XGTZ 275/40 ZR 17s in the front and huge 335/35 ZR 17s in the rear. The three-spoke wheels, similar to the design on the concept car but not as deeply dished, were painted silver.

Visual distinctions of these first-year cars include a black, external, non-power antenna mounted on the left (driver's) rear fender, an indent in the right rear fender next to the fuel door (as opposed to in the fuel door itself), four polished ribs on the intake manifold runners, and the word "Viper" imprinted on the brake calipers. Also, the battery was located under a panel inside the trunk between the frame rails for easier access and better weight distribution.

There were no factory options. Officially, air conditioning was available only as a dealer-installed option that year, though according to Al Byerle of DaimlerChrysler, four Vipers were built at the plant with A/C. The gas tank capacity was 22 gallons. The trunk was left unfinished with the spare tire and bare trunk walls exposed. Nineteen ninety-two was the only year that Viper owners received a large, zippered leather valise with the snake emblem embossed on the front that could hold the service manual, parts manual, owner's manual, and warranty booklet.

If you're interested in collecting a Viper, 1992 is a good choice because it was both the first year of production and the second lowest production year for RT/10s (1997 was the lowest). Currently, there's barely a premium on this year. However, if you're buying a Viper to drive, 1992 may not be the best year to choose. Being a first-year production car, there were some teething pains as Chrysler, a mass-production company, learned to build a limited-production vehicle. Consequently, build quality is inconsistent.

Some 1992 and early 1993 engines suffered an oil consumption problem, due to incorrect ring seating. On some cars, after several thousand miles, a mist of black oil would blow out the exhaust pipes. At the time, the service policy was to send the engines back to Detroit for rebuild or replacement. In many cases, the rebuilt engine returned to the customer was not necessarily the same block from the original car, so the numbers on the engine may not match the VIN. Though legitimate, it still may be a concern to the collector who is looking for a "numbers-matching" car, so be sure to obtain documentation if the engine is not original.

If you're buying a 1992, particularly a low-mileage "museum" car, the oil problem may not have been detected or corrected and you may end up having to deal with a rebuild.

Early cars used a rigid exhaust hanger which could rattle. Many were retrofitted to the later style spring mount.

Viper Specifications 1992–1995 RT/10	
Engine	8.0 L V-10
Bore/Stroke	4.00" x 3.88"
Power (bhp @ rpm)	400 @ 4,600
Torque (lb-ft @ rpm*	465 @ 3600
Compression Ratio	9.1:1
Transmission	6-spd manual
Final Drive	3.07:1
Wheelbase	96.2"
Track (front/rear)	59.6"/60.6"
Overall Length	175.1"
Overall Width	75.7"
Overall Height	43.9"
Curb Weight	3456 lbs
Weight distribution	50/50
Ground Clearance	5.0"
Coefficient of Drag (cd)	0.495
Fuel Tank Capacity	22 gallons
Engine Oil	9 quarts
Frame	Tubular space frame
Front Suspension	Independent, unequal length A-arms
Front Shocks	Coil-over, low pressure gas Adjustable rebound
Front Anti-roll Bar	Tubular 27 mm diameter
Rear Suspension	Independent, unequal length A-arms
Rear shocks	Coil-over, low pressure gas Adjustable rebound
Rear Anti-roll bar	Tubular 22 mm diameter
Steering	Power rack & pinion
Front Brakes	13" vented discs with 4-piston calipers
Rear Brakes	13" vented discs with single piston calipers
Front Wheels	10" x 17" cast aluminum
Rear Wheels	13" x 17" cast aluminum
Front Tires	Michelin XGT 275/40 ZR17
Rear Tires	Michelin XGT 335/35 ZR17
Tire pressure	35 psi
Notes	* torque rated between 450 & 485 lb-ft

I Bought a 1992 Viper

Phil Eiselin bought his 1992 Viper when it was less than a year old and has owned it ever since. Phil is a car nut and Harley fan from way-back, and was the Fleet Manager at a Dodge dealer at the time.

I first saw the Viper on the cover of Road & Track in 1989. It was pure magic—that voluptuous body, that hourglass figure, and that aggressive front end. Finally, here was a car with personality. For me, it's the only car, even today, that looking at still makes my heart beat faster.

The first night I took my wife Vicky to dinner, she was wearing a skirt with nylons and promptly melted them on the exhaust. Being used to riding on a Harley, her only comment was, "I guess I'm going to have to wear pants, just like on the Harley, so I don't burn my legs on the exhaust."

Driving the Viper fast demands all of your attention, since torque is available even at low rpm. I use it as my personal "shrink." After a hard day at work, it's nice to take the car out to get an "attitude adjustment" and clear your mind of all your problems.

Ninety-two was the first year, so there were some teething problems with fit and finish. My engine started blowing oil at about 8,500 miles. First, the dealer tried to replace the rings in the engine. But that didn't last, so at about 20,000 miles, I had to send the engine back to Detroit for a rebuild. They sent back a 1994 engine instead of my original 1992 engine. After some insistence, I eventually got my original engine back—rebuilt. If you're going to buy a 1992 or early 1993, I recommend looking for a car that has all the engine updates.

92 RT/10 *Chrysler*

What They Said in 1992

The Viper turns heads.

It elicits whoops and hollers of approval. A pair of young Turks in a Toyota MR2 let loose with a lusty catcall of the sort usually reserved for the L.A. Lakers cheerleaders. A middle-aged couple in a Bronco with Indiana plates pull up alongside and flash the thumbs up sign. A biker who could pass for one of the Grateful Dead chugs his Harley even with the Viper to cut a gap-toothed smile and a nod of recognition. "Dig it man, the Harley Hog of sports cars."

The Viper sits low and wide, as if ready to uncoil with explosive force at a moments notice. At 75.7 in., it's wider than a Corvette ZR-1 or Ferrari 348. Standing just 44.0 in. high, the Viper squats lower than a Ferrari F-40 or Testarossa and more than 2 in. lower than the Acura NSX.

And though every dimension and body panel have been changed to meet federal safety regulations or production-line realities, the Viper remains true to the form of the original show-stopper that wowed 'em on the Chrysler turntable at the 1989 North American International Auto Show in Detroit.

One of the goals foremost in the minds of Chrysler engineers was the Cobra's vaunted 1–100–0 miles per hour time of 15.0 sec. The Viper guys claim their snake can do it in 14.5 sec. But let's not kid ourselves. The Viper isn't about numbers. It's about unbridled emotion on wheels. It's about explosive locomotion and the power to blast to 100 or 150 miles per hour at will without working up a sweat. It's about balance and a 50/50 weight distribution that lets a skilled driver arm-wrestle difficult corners, approach and dance on the edge of the laws of physics without computer intervention.

Chrysler President Bob Lutz summed it up this way, "Viper is not for everyone. This car is only for the enthusiast who wants a great driving car and nothing more."

~*Road & Track*, February 1992

The windows don't roll up. Matter of fact, there are no windows. Or outside door handles. Not much protection against the weather, either—the "top" is simply a section of canvas that stretches from the windshield header to the "sport bar." There is no hardtop.

But what there is in this Dodge Viper RT/10 is a ten-cylinder, 488-cubic-inch powerplant producing 400 horsepower and a *Car and Driver*-measured 13.2 second quarter-mile time that makes it quicker than the altogether outrageous Chevrolet Corvette ZR-1.

And with the wind ripping new configurations in your eyebrows and the engine in full honk, you're not going to give one whit about absent windows or door handles. Because this Viper is one of the most exciting rides since Ben Hur discovered the chariot.

It is nicely balanced, with a little polite understeer most of the time, and the Michelin XGT-Zs' breakaway is not particularly sudden . . . It even rides well, with minimal harshness and a sense of tremendous structural rigidity.

The engine makes so much power and the tires generate so much grip that the car can work up tremendous speed without sweat or drama, and that could prove deceptive. High limits, once they're exceeded, mean big trouble.

Yet isn't that much of the appeal? Not the danger itself, but the awesome potential, the no-foolin' manner—those same qualities that demand respect also make a machine like this irresistible.

~*Car and Driver*, March 1992

Indy Pace Car Replicas

When it was announced that the Dodge Stealth R/T would serve as the pace car for the Indy 500 in 1991, an uproar occurred because the Stealth was a Japanese-built car made by Mitsubishi. A prototype Viper RT/10 was called into duty instead. Since Viper production didn't begin until the following year, no Indy Pace Car replicas were ever built by the factory. However, Dodge's answer was to release 50 sets of pace car decals, which could be purchased separately for $100. Since the actual pace car didn't require any mechanical modifications (except for strobe lights), any 1992 or 1993 red Viper RT/10 with the pace car decals can be considered a pace car replica.

Decals could be purchased to transform any 1992–1993 RT/10 into an Indy Pace Car replica.

1992 and early 1993 engines were prone to oil consumption due to improper ring seating. Check if car has had an engine rebuild because of this and, if so, if the VIN on the block still matches the chassis' VIN. If no engine rebuild was done, check that the car does not blow oil.

Four-rib intake manifold.

Twin throttle body cables require periodic adjustment to maintain correct synchronization and maximum throttle opening, and to reduce jerking motions at slow speeds.

If car runs hot, check if the cooling system has been properly flushed, filled, and "burped" to remove all the air. The filling point is not the highest point in the system, so air can become trapped in the system if not properly bled.

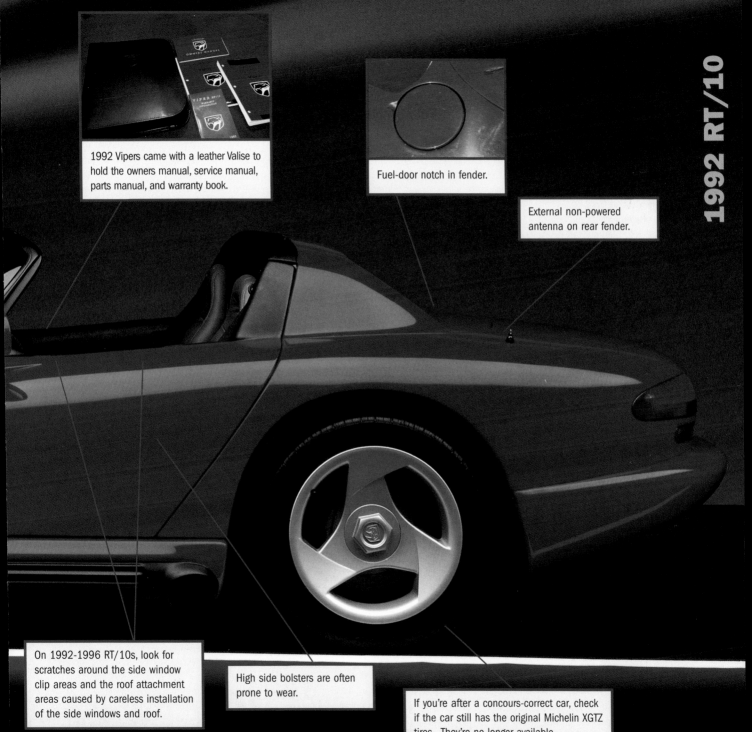

1992 Vipers came with a leather Valise to hold the owners manual, service manual, parts manual, and warranty book.

Fuel-door notch in fender.

External non-powered antenna on rear fender.

On 1992-1996 RT/10s, look for scratches around the side window clip areas and the roof attachment areas caused by careless installation of the side windows and roof.

High side bolsters are often prone to wear.

If you're after a concours-correct car, check if the car still has the original Michelin XGTZ tires. They're no longer available.

1993 RT/10

Collectibility: ✱✱✱

Production of 1993 Viper RT/10 began on December 14, 1992. Black was added to the color choices, and VIN 1 was built as a black roadster and retained for use by Dodge Marketing as a show car. Early 1993 roadsters were just a continuation of the 1992 model. Around VIN 605 (May of 1993) several significant changes were made:

Hidden antenna: The radio antenna was changed from the left rear fender to being molded into the windshield. This change was primarily made to meet international safety regulations, but it also made for a cleaner look and made it easier to cover the car.

Reverse lockout added: An electronic reverse lockout was added to the transmission to prevent drivers from accidentally engaging reverse when shifting into fifth.

Battery location changed: The battery was moved from between the rear frame rails to outside the left frame rail on all Vipers to make space for the rear-exit exhausts used on the export cars.

What They Said in 1993

The sun was shining again, and that is the weather to enjoy your Viper, a pleasure machine if ever there was one. The best thing is that it is purpose-built, with almost no compromises. If you need power windows, power seats, ABS, air bags, a power top or air conditioning, the Viper is not for you. It has been designed to go, and God it goes! Anything that might reduce the ability of the world's most voluminous passenger car engine to make the Viper go fast—that means anything that adds weight—has been ruthlessly banned. If that is not your idea of a sports car, then buy a Corvette or a Stealth. They are nice, fast cars you can even go shopping with, but they lack the excitement the Viper can provide.

And what fascinates me most is the car's overtaking ability. You choose the right gear, wait until the road is clear, and as soon as you depress the accelerator, you get an immediate mammoth kick in the back that catapults you past the vehicle to be overtaken.

Maybe some of the better turbo-charged production sports cars can produce similar acceleration, but it inevitably takes some time to build up. With the Viper's huge atmospherically aspirated engine, the acceleration is right there, instantly reflecting the orders given by the right foot, and that puts the performance into a completely different perspective.

Both American and European specification Vipers were made available to me on this journey, but the differences are minimal and limited to those required by laws or practicality, such as the different seatbelt systems, the rear rather than side-exhaust system of the European version and its instruments calibrated in metric units. And in Europe, the car is a Chrysler, not a Dodge.
~*Road & Track*, February 1993

Are there cars out there that are as much fun to drive as the Dodge Viper? Maybe, but it's an awfully short list, and unlike the competition, the Viper's novelty and star appeal still are there.

Sure, there are deficiencies. Viper doesn't have the fit and finish some competitors have. The frame welds look like a high school auto shop project. Hot air blows constantly into the footwell, roasting feet and legs like turkey drumsticks. The "top" is woefully inadequate and as difficult to manage as the worst on the old British roadsters. There is room for exactly two people and maybe one paper-thin piece of luggage. But who cares?

This is a Viper, not a Honda Accord. It's not supposed to be practical, it's supposed to be fun. And is it ever.
~*AutoWeek*, July 5, 1993

A list of our favorite (fun cars) includes the adrenal acceleration rush of a Porsche 911 Turbo, the contentment of a topless Mazda Miata on a sunny country road, the way heads turn our way when we're behind the wheel of a Ferrari 512TR, the thrill of carving up a back road in a Mazda RX7, and the nostalgic dreams of a Shelby Cobra. The Viper combines the best of these, and adds its own special touches. As a result, it swamped our subjective fun-factor voting, earning first-place points from three of five voting editors.

"A very good track car—stable and predictable with tremendous grip," said one editor. "This is a play toy, not a real car," said one editor. "And I like it for that reason."
~*Motor Trend*, June 1993

New top- and-side curtain material: The top and side curtain material was changed from a pebble-grain vinyl to a more cloth-like material called "Hartz."

Air conditioning was still a dealer-installed option. During this time, Chrysler was negotiating rights to the Viper name with an auto alarm company, so the imprint on the front brake calipers changed from "Viper" to "RT/10." The finger-access notch for the fuel filler door was moved from the fender to the fuel door itself, presumably to make it easier to finish the fender. A yellow "caution" zone was added to the coolant temperature gauge just below the maximum temperature. The large leather valises were changed to a smaller black cover that contained the owner's manual, warranty information, and the hubcap removal tool.

Hood production problems limited 1993 production to only 1043, making it the second lowest year in *total* Viper production. Despite this rarity, prices on the 1993 roadsters are usually the lowest, making it one of the best buys for a Viper right now.

I Bought a 1993 Viper

I'm probably the ultimate Viperholic. Heck, I even coined the phrase. So here's your author's story:

I remember the exact moment I fell in love with the Viper. It was between the mailbox and the front door, looking at the Viper concept car on the cover of the April '89 issue of *Road & Track*. As I walked through the front door, I announced to my girlfriend, "If they build this, I'll buy it!"

I was too young to experience the muscle car era first hand, so at the time, I had a classic Dodge Challenger R/T. I also had a Porsche. With the Viper, I could have both the acceleration of a classic American musclecar along with the handling of a European sports car, all wrapped in a drop-dead gorgeous body. And it would be so impractical; you'd have to be a car nut to own one. I wrote to Chrysler, begging them to put it in production, and promising to buy one. From then on, I followed the Viper like it was my own pet project, collecting every piece of information I could get my hands on.

In 1992, I registered as a journalist for the Detroit auto show so I could attend the unveiling of the new Viper. I couldn't afford the ridiculous dealer markups on the 1992s, so I ordered one from a sympathetic dealer who agreed to sell me one at sticker price. And then I waited. And waited. For 16 months.

It was worth the wait. The Viper is unlike any other exotic/sports/muscle car. It accelerates *right now*. No waiting. You'd better be sure that the space you're headed for is open, because before you can think, you're there. And contrary to what BMW and NSX owners like to think, the car is not just a straight-line muscle car. It corners as well. Here's a clue. Have you looked at how wide those rear tires are?

It's like having your own amusement park ride. Driving the Viper is such a raw, visceral experience. Ford had a commercial that asked, "Have you ever asked the road to dance?" There's no better partner than the Viper RT/10. Nothing puts a smile on your face like driving the roadster down your favorite twisty back road on a warm, sunny day. And the experiences I've had in life and the wonderful friends I've made all around the world are all because of the Viper.

I've had the good fortune to own or drive some wonderful cars—muscle cars, Porsches, Ferraris, and Lamborghinis—but the original "classic" Viper roadster is still my favorite. After 10 years and over 100,000 miles in my Vipers, they're still my favorite car. And the best part is, they're affordable—to buy and maintain—especially now. So, if you're a serious car nut, just do it!

Owner's manual cover was reduced to fit in the glove box. It also holds the hubcap removal tool.

Rearview mirror lowered slightly for better view through sport bar.

Hidden antenna in windshield.

Look for scrape marks on front spoiler.

Check for brittle spark plug wires. Engine heat can cause wires to break down in less than 20,000 miles.

Brake calipers changed to read "RT/10."

Temp gauge gets yellow caution zone.

Fuel door notch moved from fender to the door.

Battery moved to outside of left frame rail. Changing the battery requires removing the left rear wheel and fender liner. (Battery jump-start post is up front in engine compartment.)

All vents in rear valence are cut out.

Check for heavy clutch-pedal feel on higher mileage cars (over 50,000 miles). Clutch effort increases as the clutch wears.

Tires typically last about 25,000 miles.

The only interior color choice for the first two years was gray.

Ron Kimball

1994 RT/10

Collectibility: **

By 1994, most of the production glitches had been ironed out and production reached an all-time high of 3083 units. The big news for 1994 was the addition of two colors to the palette: Dandelion Yellow (PJE), a solid, bright yellow, and Emerald Green Pearl Coat (PGQ), a metallic dark teal-green color. Red and black continued to be available. The three-spoke wheels were now painted a brighter metallic silver—something to watch out for if you're purchasing replacement three-spoke wheels.

There were several changes inside the Viper as well. An optional tan interior was available with tan-colored seats and carpet and a black dash. Air conditioning was now available as a factory-installed option for $1200.

What They Said in 1994

Automobile Magazine readers voted Viper the car you'd most like a friend to buy so you could cruise around in it without having to own it; best car for those in need of attention; best car for a burnout the length of Main Street.

~*Automobile Magazine*, August 1994

It pulled up next to me at a light, and I actually let out a moan. "Whooaagh," I said from my diaphragm. My first encounter with a Dodge Viper RT/10.

I was taken with that Viper. Waiting at the light, I studied it, running my eyes over its smooth lines and voluptuous curves. I wondered about the guy behind the wheel: What is it like to be him, to drive such an outrageous road machine? How does it feel to have schleps like me trundling around town in our blue Tempos, staring at your car with lustful envy? . . .

At work the next day, I told my editor about the story he had to let me write. "Of course," I told him, "I'd have to drive one." A visionary with keen story sense, he approved, simply saying, "Make sure they have insurance."

I feel like I've just gotten away with a huge prank. I've just stolen this car for a joy ride. Alex (the Chrysler PR guy) never even asked to see my driver's license. I had to go through a more rigorous check for a Heineken.

It's a drug, I almost say out loud. This car is a drug. Last night I dreamed about sixth gear. On a race track, I had room to go fast enough to use sixth gear. Fifty thousand fans cheered as I took the checkered flag.

I feel the drug now. We go rampaging through sleepy countryside at seventy, eighty, twice the speed limit, tearing around blind corners. People come out to their mailboxes and give us the thumbs up and smile like we've just liberated Michigan from the occupation forces. If you've never driven through small-town America in a big, yellow, American muscle car with the top down and the radio blaring, then I highly recommend it.

I bust out early and hit I-696 again. This time alone, determined to reach sixth gear. At this speed, I have to squint against the wind vortexes whipping through the cockpit. At twice the speed of the other cars, it seems as if they're parked on the highway. I feel like I'm speed-skating on an ice rink filled with children just learning. I am a yellow blur, and I am high.

I feel slightly strung out. That's what it's like, I realize. That's how the guy at the red light feels. He drives that Viper so schleps like me will stare, so people will wave and smile. He drives with the top down so the sun can shine on his face while he listens to the radio and ten cylinders sucking up gas. And every time he sees an open stretch of road, he has a jones for sixth gear.

~*American Way*, November 1994

Customers with earlier cars had expressed concern when their temperature indicators often reached the yellow caution zone. Team Viper felt that the temperature was acceptable, so they simply removed the yellow warning zone from the gauge.

Under the hood, a simpler-construction intake manifold (identified by three-ribs) replaced the four-rib one. And now that Chrysler had resolved the issue of using the "Viper" name, the word "Viper" returned to the brake calipers around late calendar year 1994 (some 1995s still used "RT/10").

The MSRP crept up from the original $52,800 to $54,500 (plus gas guzzler and destination charge).

Nineteen ninety-four and 1995 are a couple of the best years for early roadsters because the plant had worked out the glitches in the manufacturing process and build quality was improved.

I Bought a 1994 Viper

Wayne Wenger collects classic cars, but the Viper caught his attention and is the only "new" car in his collection. Why?

At age 11, I was a car nut and building balsa models of the Jaguar 120 and the 1950 Nash Healeys. In 1955, I entered GM's Fisher Body Craftsman contest, hoping to get a scholarship. I entered again in 1959 and won a T-shirt and a $25 check, but not the scholarship.

Now, I have a stable of 10 early-1950s American muscle/sports cars—cars like the Muntz Road Jet, and the Cord. But the crown jewel is my Viper RT/10. What a car!

I was so excited when Dodge showed the Viper prototype in 1989. A modern version of the '50s exotic roadster was finally here. I was even willing to sell all my cars to purchase one at the $45,000 projected price. Unfortunately, by the time the car was introduced, the actual price had escalated to over $60,000, so my dream fell apart. But I kept reading about the car, and when Dodge added yellow and emerald green as new colors in 1994, my eyes really opened up. Especially with the tan interior. This combination was going to be my choice if I ever purchased a Viper.

In 2002, my dream finally came true. I saw my dream Viper for sale in Hemmings. It was emerald green with a tan interior and had only 20,000 miles on it. One thing led to another, and I purchased the car—which was in Cincinnati, OH. I talked my son-in-law into flying there and driving the Viper back with me, along a route parallel to Route 66.

What a ball—driving that fire-breathing snake across the country. Many drivers wanted to race us, but we were just getting acquainted with the Viper. I love the fact that it has no exterior door handles, that it has sidepipes, a removable rear window, side curtains, a removable top, seats that conform to your back, and simple, aircraft-style-instruments. And of course, the torque from that 400-horsepower V-10 engine is great for mountain roads.

Above all, I love that great look! The fish-gill front fenders as they meet the doors. The smooth headlights and tail. When you see a Viper in person, you see one of the most distinctive car designs of this decade. Nothing beats a Viper look.

Factory-installed A/C.

Optional factory hardtops like the one shown on this car became available in 1995 and could be retrofitted to older cars.

Optional black and tan interior.

Look for curb scrapes on wheels, particularly the right rear wheels. Unidirectional design and different front/rear sizes mean that wheels are not interchangeable. Right rear three-spoke wheels are becoming harder to find as this is the most often damaged wheel.

1994 wheels were painted a brighter silver color. "Viper" reappeared on calipers in late 1994–early 1995.

No yellow warning zone in temperature gauge.

New, simpler-construction three-rib intake manifold.

Maurice Q. Liang

1995 RT/10

Collectibility: ✳✳✳

Nineteen ninety-five was the final year of the "classic" sidepipe roadster. Production dropped back down to 1,577 units, as the plant prepared to move to a new location and tool up for the revised 1996 RT/10 and the new GTS coupe.

The same color choices were available for 1995—red, black, yellow, and green, as well as the choice of gray or tan interior. Inside, a much-needed grab handle was added to the passenger door, and responding to comments about limited storage space in the cockpit, Team Viper added storage pockets to the front of the seat cushions. An insulation pad with the Viper snake emblem embossed in it was added under the hood.

A double-bubble hardtop, designed to mimic the roofline of the forthcoming GTS coupe, was now available as a factory option for $2,500. The top was made by supplier ASC and was designed to work with the factory side curtains, whereas many aftermarket tops required the use of their own matching side curtains. Lucky owners who attended the second Viper Owner's Invitational in Monterey, CA, received the $2,500 hardtop as a gift from Dodge.

It was no secret that the sidepipes were going away for 1996, so the factory commemorated the last of the sidepipe cars by putting a stamp on the toe box under the hood on the last 300 cars built. While a nice touch, at this point, it adds little to the actual value of the car.

I Bought a 1995 Viper

Can you really drive a Viper RT/10 on a daily basis? Owner Randy Davis does:

Many people look in disbelief when I tell them I drive mine daily, especially other Viper owners who can't conceive of leaving their baby out of their sight unless it is in the garage. I just couldn't see paying this much for a car and not driving it. I've driven my Viper daily since buying the car five years ago and have racked up some 65,000 miles—including two trips between California and Oklahoma. The rewards of driving it on a daily basis as well as a multi-day highway trip are well worth it. It gives a whole new meaning to wanting to drive to work and is often my first thought when waking up in the morning—"I get to drive the Viper to work!" However, I must confess I still shared the view of not really wanting to let it out of my sight in a public place for a long period of time. So, having an office that overlooks a fairly unused section of parking lot made things a lot easier.

Being a motorcyclist prepared me well for the challenges of driving a first-generation Viper—no windows or any way to lock the car (until I bought some aftermarket lockable windows from Northwind Engineering), watching the weather closely so I wouldn't get caught in the rain (more because I didn't want to wash it than anything else), and generally dealing with driving a vehicle with an extremely high power-to-weight ratio. Though, compared with riding a motorcycle, driving a Viper is pure luxury—it's more comfortable, plus I have air conditioning!

What They Said in 1995

(A couple of views from the other side of the pond, as they say.)

"Is that a car?" asked a young lad dressed in shorts and wellies as the Viper rumbled slowly past. "Look at one of those, Dad!" squawked another across the street as the three test cars rolled slowly by in close convoy.

The first nipper can be forgiven for spouting such an obvious question. It doesn't matter whether you're nine or 90, the first time you see a Viper on the road . . . you're likely to lose control of your faculties. Words can be uttered over which your brain has absolutely no control.

The second boy gave himself a nanosecond between actually catching sight of the cars and spluttering the words he did. It matters not that he may have already been familiar with the shapes of the 911 or the SL, the Viper stole the show instantaneously—and he knew it would for his Dad, too.

On the road, you'll be aware that the Viper is a no-frills, back-to-basics machine. Sure, there's an excellent air conditioning system which keeps you comfortable and prevents the somewhat drab interior from misting up when it's wet and the top and sidescreens are in place, and there's a reasonable Alpine stereo in the dash, too. But that's about it.

Anyone much shorter than six foot will have trouble depressing the clutch pedal fully, and the enormous transmission tunnel encroaches on elbow space. The huge, badly positioned rear view mirror obstructs your view of the road ahead on right handers. The Viper leaves you physically and mentally drained. Keeping the car on the left-hand side of the road requires frenzied, unfailing effort—and that's not just because of its massive width. It is this more or less constant nervousness which has prevented us all from remortgaging our houses.

As sports car enthusiasts, we are bound to conclude that, although the Viper is truly a wonderful brute of a car, most of the British Isles are either too bumpy or too crowded for it. We love the Viper, but we'd find it hard to deal with on a regular basis.

Top Gear Magazine, January 1995, comparing the Viper with a Mercedes SL and Porsche 911 Cabriolet in the United Kingdom

A simultaneous racing start from these leviathans (the Viper and the Lamborghini LM002) would almost certainly upset the planet's rotational velocity. The Dodge Viper is to motoring, what a sledge hammer is to a walnut. On paper, the Viper might appear to be a point and squirt dragster. The truth is that the handling is better than you might imagine and the engine worse.

The Viper's muscle-bound body and the Lamborghini's macho bulges can turn some people on as much as they can turn others off. Vulgar or voluptuous, you choose.

Zero–60 miles per hour takes 4.5 seconds and 100 miles per hour comes up in 14.5 seconds. Such is the power delivery, that it feels more like a runaway jet aircraft than a sports car. What impressed me most was the handling. Preconceptions of poor US handling abounded. How could a truck-engined boulevardier's dragster possibly cope with Goodwood Circuit? Well it did. The four massive ventilated discs arrest the Viper quickly and without undue suspension dive. One hundred miles per hour to zero in 4.6 seconds is serious stopping power. Just ask Isaac Newton. With well sorted double wishbone independent suspension at each corner, coil-over shocks and two anti-roll bars mounted to a strong tubular steel space-frame, the Viper is in the exclusive 1g cornering club. Acceleration away from an apex is impressive. Body roll and chassis flex remained low while wind buffeting felt like ten rounds with Frank Bruno.

~*AutoItalia*, comparing the Viper to the Lamborghini LM002 SUV, 1995

Seat cushion storage pockets added.

Check weather-stripping around trunk for wear.

Rear valence vents no longer cut out.

Last 300 sidepipe stamping on toe box, under the hood.

Underhood insulation pad added.

On yellow cars, the fog light cavity was masked off before painting to leave it black.

Side-exit exhaust covers are prone to scrapes on all 1992-1995 RT/10s and are expensive to replace.

Passenger grab handle added. The grab handle was not available as a separate part. To retrofit an older car with one, the entire door panel had to be replaced.

On yellow cars, the area behind the grill on the hood were painted black to improve the appearance.

Ron Kimball

Collectibility: ✶✶✶✶

Nineteen ninety-six was a year of many changes for the Viper. First, the New Mack Avenue Assembly Plant was being converted to an engine plant, so the Viper found a new home at the Conner Avenue Assembly Plant (CAAP), still in Detroit.

In addition, the GTS coupe, with its new body, chassis, and engine, was due to debut—but not until mid-1996. Dodge decided to build the 1996 roadsters for the first half of the year and then switch completely to building the GTS coupe to fill the huge first-year demand. Consequently, RT/10 production was only 721 for 1996.

The 1996 RT/10 was a transitional car. Team Viper gave the roadster the new lighter and stiffer chassis with cast-aluminum A-arms, cast-aluminum five-spoke wheels, Michelin Pilot MXX3 SX tires, and rear-exit exhaust (with smooth side sills) from the forthcoming coupe, but retained the original body, interior, and engine. Engine horsepower was increased slightly from 400 to 415 horsepower, and torque was up from 465 lb-ft to 488 lb-ft, mostly due to reduced back pressure in the exhaust system.

To improve the quality and yield of the large clamshell hoods, the Viper's hood was now made using sheet molded compound (SMC) instead of the old resin transfer molding (RTM) method. The trunk was enlarged slightly to allow for a cutout in the back wall for the spare tire well, which reduced the fuel tank capacity from 22 to 19 gallons. The cooling system was also upgraded. Side curtains with sliding and lockable hard-plastic windows replaced the soft zip-up windows.

With the new chassis, suspension tuning, and Michelin Pilot tires, the Viper had less knife-edge handling limits. Depending on your driving style and experience, this could be a good thing or a bad thing. Also, the ride was more compliant and the new Michelin tires greatly improved wet weather traction.

The most noticeable changes were the color choices. Originally, Team Viper planned to do one "special edition" Viper for 1996. Three styling proposals were developed for management to review: an all-American white with blue stripes body with white wheels and blue steering wheel, handbrake grip, and shift knob; a "Harley-look" black with silver stripes and silver wheels; and a "Ferrari-look" red with yellow wheels and emblems and red shift knob, handbrake grip, and steering wheel (affectionately referred to as the "McViper"). All had black interiors. Instead of choosing one, management decided to build all three as the lineup for 1996.

People either loved them or hated them, with most being in the latter group. Some buyers went as far as replacing the red-accented interior trim and yellow wheels on their "McVipers" just to get a plain red roadster, since you could not buy a plain red roadster that year. The white with blue stripes was the most popular at 324 units, followed by the black at 231 units and the red at 166 units. But, as is often the case, the more wild the colors, the more collectible they become over time.

This was also the first time stripes appeared on the roadster. The only other time would be in 1997. Unlike the GTS, the stripes started on the hood, went across the sport cap, and stopped at the end of the deck lid. This simplified manufacturing, because the plant would not have to match the stripes on the hood and trunk to the front and rear fascias. Hardtops did not come from the factory with stripes, though many owners added these.

Viper Specifications 1996 RT/10	
Engine	8.0 L V-10
Bore/Stroke	4.00" x 3.88"
Power (bhp @ rpm)	415 @ 5200
Torque (lb-ft @ rpm*	488 @ 3600
Compression Ratio	9.1:1
Transmission	6-spd manual
Final Drive	3.07:1
Wheelbase	96.2"
Track (front/rear)	59.6"/60.6"
Overall Length	175.1"
Overall Width	75.7"
Overall Height	43.9"
Curb Weight	3445 lbs
Weight distribution	50/50
Ground Clearance	5.0"
Coefficient of Drag (cd)	0.495
Fuel Tank Capacity	19 gallons
Engine Oil	9 quarts
Frame	Tubular space frame
Front Suspension	Independent, unequal length A-arms
Front Shocks	Coil-over, low pressure gas Adjustable rebound
Front Anti-roll Bar	Tubular 27 mm diameter
Rear Suspension	Independent, unequal length A-arms
Rear shocks	Coil-over, low pressure gas Adjustable rebound
Rear Anti-roll bar	Tubular 22 mm diameter
Steering	Power rack & pinion
Front Brakes	13" vented discs with 4-piston calipers
Rear Brakes	13" vented discs with single piston calipers
Front Wheels	10" x 17" cast aluminum
Rear Wheels	13" x 17" cast aluminum
Front Tires	Michelin Pilot SX 275/40 ZR17
Rear Tires	Michelin Pilot SX 335/35 ZR17
Tire pressure	29 psi

The stripes were made from a 3M film instead of paint to give a more consistent and repeatable color. The body panel was first color-coated and clear-coated, and it was wet-sanded. The stripes were applied using a laser alignment system, and then the panel was clear-coated again.

As time goes on, the challenge becomes finding the unique replacement parts for these cars, like the blue or red interior trim pieces. As an interesting side note, the wheels on the black car were intended to be polished, but the cast-aluminum wheels proved difficult to polish, so they were painted silver instead.

I Bought a 1996 Viper

Dreams come true. Can you relate to Curtis Ratica's story?

I have fantasized about sports cars since I was a child. There were all the muscle cars, the Trans-Ams, the Camaros, the Superbird, and of course the almighty Corvette. Ferrari was the ultimate car for any child, but it seemed more like a distant dream rather than something just out of reach, like the Corvette. After all, you saw Corvettes nearly everyday, and the neighbor down the street had one. That was certainly attainable one day, when I got out of school and got a job.

I was 23 years old when I got my Corvette—a black '84. I loved that car, but after a lot of problems, I finally sold it. I wanted more. I wanted an exotic.

After looking at all types of sports cars in the $50,000 range, I narrowed it down to three cars: The Viper RT/10 or GTS, the 1963–1967 Corvette roadster, or any Ferrari in that price range. I finally decided on the Viper because a) it looks awesome, b) it has world-class power, and c) it has world-class handling. After a couple of months of searching, I found an original-owner 1996 white with blue stripes RT/10 with only 10,800 miles.

After the car was delivered and I had signed all the paperwork, I sat in my car and just tried to breathe. I was too excited. I was in awe at the beauty of this beast and it was mine! Finally, at last, I have an exotic, a Viper, a world-class supercar! I strapped myself in and thought to myself how tight everything was. It felt like I was in a race car. Then I started the car. It rumbled, it shook, it sounded great!

My adrenaline was pumping. I couldn't wait to go but I was a little . . . umm . . . afraid . . . at the same time. The car launched smoothly and I began driving down an open road with few other cars in sight. It felt absolutely terrific. I had to climb a steep hill on the way home so I thought it would be a great place to apply a bit of throttle. I did and it responded—by breaking the rear tires loose and drifting sideways a little.

Having owned the car for about a year now, I have found the car to be very easy to drive and very controllable. If you get on it a lot, and especially if the car is not pointing perfectly straight ahead, it can get out from underneath you. There's just nothing like it. It's as close to driving a race car on the street as you'll find. The overall world-class performance is amazing. The power, speed, handling, and looks all work together to create a sensational driving experience. The torque will pin you to your seat to stay. The handling is wonderful and the ride is much smoother than expected.

Aside from a pressure release valve in the fuel tank, I have had zero problems with the car. The only drawbacks are, being King of the Hill, you will always have people wanting to race you, and some people will be jealous and will try their best to put down your car. And, it's a productivity waster. You'll spend a lot of time staring at your car, cleaning your car, or just thinking about staring at or cleaning your car.

Despite being a person who is always looking for something a little better, I think it's safe to say I will have a Viper for a long, long time. For the money, there isn't anything close to the Viper in terms of beauty, driving experience, world-class handling, and sheer power. The closest competition is about $200,000 away.

What They Said in 1996

Driving the 1996 RT/10 is an exhilarating experience, and the difference between this car and last year's model is like night and day. The harsh bump steer and erratic tracking characteristics of the original Viper have been nearly done away with, vastly improving one's sense of confidence and control.

The new suspension and tire combination definitely works to the car's advantage in handling and ride quality, where increased stick and decreased slither are the new orders of the day. One is still advised to pay strict attention to the business of driving, however; no matter how many upgrades one foists upon this car it's still a 400+ horse serpent that you've got by the tail, and things are bound to happen quickly.

~*Sports Car International*, September 1995

When other cars were getting their diplomas from finishing school, the Viper was out dodging the truancy officer. But like any street-smart kid, it made up for its lack of polish in ways no other car could ever hope to emulate.

Case in point: Crack open the twin throttle bodies with your right foot, and the sort of thrust known previously to astronauts, fighter jocks, and human cannonballs is yours. The enormous 8.0-liter pushrod V-10 might seem crude in mechanical specification, but its execution is first-class—a steel-sleeved aluminum block developed with the help of Lamborghini, forged connecting rods and crankshaft, and a mild camshaft with minimal overlap for docile low-rev operation.

The 1996 Viper is quicker than the 1995 model and, believe you me, can out-thunder almost anything short of a 12-cylinder Italian exotic or Porsche 911 Turbo through the quarter mile. How about 12.9 seconds past the timing lights? Or 4.6 seconds to 60 miles per hour? The Ferrari F40 and Vector W8, each orders of magnitude more expensive, are the only rear-drive production cars listed in our Road Test Summary that can trounce it. When its engine is on full boil, there is something so utterly unstoppable about this car; a backroom deal seems to have been made to bend the laws of physics here.

But changes here have charmed the snake, lending a more agile feel and causing less apprehension as the limit is approached. Cornering is so flat and tires are so quiet that you'd almost welcome more roll and squeal. But if you patiently work to the edge of the envelope, the big Dodge rewards with precision, sure-footedness and 0.96g of seat bolster-compressing grip.

~*Road & Track*, November 1995

Roy Sjoberg is the executive engineer on the Viper and has been in charge ever since December of 1988. He headed the team that turned that show car into a no-kidding-folks reality. He also describes himself as my "former girlfriend's little-shit kid brother," referring to a time back when the surface of the earth was cooling and I was going out with his beautiful sister, Joan. I also raced sports cars with one of Roy's two half-brothers, Bob Steele. As they say, Roy Sjoberg and I go back a ways.

I've known Carroll Shelby, the spiritual father of the Viper, almost as long as I've known Roy Sjoberg, having met him in the mid-1950s when he tried to run over me while traveling backward at about 70 miles per hour in the rain in Tony Parravano's 3.5 Ferrari. Bob Lutz, the official father of the Viper, lives nearby in Ann Arbor and has been known to drive one or another of his own classic cars over to Larry Crane's house where we occasionally gather for mornings of coffee and bench racing.

Bob Lutz offered me my first ride in a Viper prototype one summer night. We went very quickly around a long demonstration circuit . . . then brought the car back to the tent . . . where the Viper promptly caught fire. It was Roy Sjoberg who came trotting out of the tent with a pitcher of ice water, with which he extinguished the small blaze, caused by a rear tire rubbing on a body panel. Thus, from all this, you can see why I feel a certain kinship with the Viper.

I have enjoyed several good drives in production Vipers, and two that were absolutely breathtaking. It was on one of these two, a very fast run through the northern California hills in company with Dr. Lou Sellyei in his Ferrari 250 Testa Rossa, that the idea of owning a Viper first came to me. It is exactly my kind of car—faster than most, stable as the Swiss franc, and a genuine pleasure to drive. Then I attended the introduction of the new Viper GTS coupe at Pebble Beach, and there were several proto-type 1996 RT/10 roadsters sitting around the greensward. The one that caught my eye was white with white wheels and blue dorsal stripes, America's racing colors, and I was sold.

I was able to drive my Viper off the end of the assembly line, and then stand by while the people who had worked on my car signed their names on the inside of its deck lid. The plant stopped building roadsters in March, in order to change over to the new GTS coupes. Plans call for a resumption of roadster production some time in the not-too-distant future, and Roy Sjoberg hopes they never stop building the open cars. Unfortunately, the sports car constituency is fickle, and, so far, only Porsche's 911, Chevrolet's Corvette, and Mazda's Miata have demonstrated any possibility of eternal life. It's difficult to imagine brand-new RT/10s rolling off the line in model year 2000, which I guess is why I ordered mine when I did.

~David E. Davis, Jr., Editor, *Automobile Magazine*, May 1996

1996 Garage Watch

Original-style interior, now all black with color-accented trim.

Larger trunk space meant smaller fuel tank capacity.

Rear exit exhaust (pipes still route through the smooth side sills).

New chassis with lighter, cast-aluminum A-arms from the GTS.

A-pillar rubber molding added to seal with new sliding side curtains.

Area behind the grill on the hood were painted black on white cars.

Old engine with slightly increased horsepower.

Stripes on the 1996 roadsters are prone to wear if the car was parked in the sun a lot.

New five-spoke cast-aluminum wheels from the GTS were painted on the RT/10s.

Fog light cavity was left black on white cars.

Chrysler

1997 RT/10

Collectibility: ★★★★ for blue with white stripes, and red with gold wheels/tan interior

★★ for red

Nineteen ninety-seven was the lowest production year for the RT/10, with only 117 being built as Dodge used most of the plant capacity to fill pent-up demand for the recently-introduced GTS coupe. Only 53 of the blue with white stripes combination were built. It's the only time an RT/10 came with full-length stripes running all the way down the front spoiler and the rear fascia. (The 1996 RT/10 stripes went only from the hood to trunk lid.) Solid red was the only other color available. This was the final year for the "smoothie" hood and original-style front fascia.

Optional yellow or sparkle gold wheels could be ordered with the red car. Only three RT/10s were built with the gold package and tan interior, making it another rare color combination. The five-spoke wheels were now forged instead of cast-aluminum, making them stronger as well as easier to polish to a mirror finish.

In addition to the new chassis introduced on the 1996 RT/10, the 1997 model received most of the rest of the updates from the GTS coupe. This included the new interior complete with redesigned seats, inboard seat belts, air bags, and adjustable pedals. Since the passenger air bag took the place of the glove box, the glove box was moved behind the center console, replacing one of the woofers. All interiors were black with body-color steering wheel, shift knob, and e-brake handle, similar to the 1996 cars.

The RT/10 now had outside door handles and power windows, making it much more useable. In 1997, the tonneau cover became an option. It changed slightly to accommodate the roll-up windows, and rather than attaching with snaps on the dash, it used a fiberglass rod and several mounts attached to the windshield pillars.

Under the hood, the RT/10 now had the same 450-horsepower engine as the coupe. The new engine featured a mechanical linkage between the two throttle bodies to eliminate the "lunching" (Chrysler's term for a jerking motion) caused when the older-style throttle bodies went out of sync as the throttle cables stretched. The RT/10 also received an upgraded cooling system.

The blue with white stripes RT/10 is one of the rarest and most desirable color combinations, making it one of the most collectible RT/10s, and with all the improvements, it's also one of the best to drive as well.

I Bought a 1997 Viper

So how does owning a Viper compare with other sports cars like Porsches, NSXs, and BMWs? Richard Fogg should know. He's owned over 60 different sports cars, including three Viper RT/10s—a 1994, an 2002, and the rare 1997 in blue with white stripes.

When I purchased my 1997 RT/10, I anticipated two major improvements over my 1994: power windows and more engine power. I was half right—as usual. The additional 50 horsepower was nice, but not that dramatic. However, the power windows transformed the car into a useable daily driver. They were easy, they sealed well, and they didn't wick moisture into the cabin like the foam molding on the earlier side curtains. For us four-season owners, they allowed comfortable top-off cold weather driving.

The biggest unexpected improvement over the 1994 was the tracking on bumpy and grooved roads. The new frame, revised suspension, and better Michelins all combined to make the car less twitchy and less apt to follow irregularities in the pavement. Not good, mind you, but better. The other big improvement was the interior. The adjustable pedals, especially considering the narrow footwell, were most welcomed. The new design and materials made the dash much more appropriate for an expensive car. Although the 1997 could hardly be called polished, it had much less of a "kit car" feel to it than the earlier Vipers.

The Viper is about as all-American as you can get. Built by an underdog, brought to life by the will of the people, honest and straightforward in its approach, and carrying a very big stick. It is a tremendously rewarding car to own, both for what it is and for what it represents.

Having owned many other cars, I notice that the Viper is a car that everybody likes. Some "American Iron" folks don't care for the "snotty over-priced euro-cars," but they all love the Viper. Some euro-car guys may not love the Viper, but by God they respect it! (And they should!)

One of my favorite Viper moments was when my wife, Janet, and I were on a Sunday drive in the Colorado mountains, heading toward the entrance to Rocky Mountain National Park. We were following an out-of-state minivan with an open sunroof. Just as we came around a curve that opened up the view to these beautiful snow-capped peaks, a young man stood up in the open sunroof, raised his camera, and took a picture of—our Viper—not the mountains! You gotta love a car that can do that.

What They Said in 1997

Like the GTS, the roadster needed dual air bags to meet passive restraint standards, so it got the revamped dashboard and center mounted three-point manual safety belts. Power windows, electric locks and adjustable pedals all came from the GTS, too. Since it was standard on the coupe, air conditioning was made standard on the RT/10, as well, though the buyer can opt to delete it.

Comfy as those features make it, the first word to describe this roadster is "faster." Just as in the GTS, the re-engineered 8.0-liter V-10 weighs 80 pounds less than the original and makes 450 horsepwoer and 490 lb-ft of torque. A run from 0-60 should take about four seconds flat, once you learn how to make a clean getaway.

The suspension geometry has been reconfigured with a lower rear roll center and less track change, which eradicates the dartiness and nibbling sensations of the old design. Spring rates are 40 pounds softer, the antiroll bars are recalibrated, and the 17-inch wheels use Michelin MXX3 tires. End result: The 1997 roadster understeers more than the old one, but not as much as the coupe.

Hard-core adherents to the original Viper philosophy may find the new car too soft and less lively. Most customers will appreciate that a bit of ride comfort and refinement hasn't resulted in a loss of performance.

"We took everything from the coupe that made sense for the roadster," Herb Helbig, Manager of Vehicle Synthesis, explained. "We were able to do what our customers said they wanted, and help the plant out at the same time."

Both the folding top and hardtop needed to be revised to seal with the new door windows, so Team Viper went a step further and simplified the installation—you need not remove the sport bar pad at the rear, but can simply insert the scissor clip and snap the rear of either top in place.

~*AutoWeek*, May 12, 1997

Call us heathens, but we can't help but wonder how the nasty Cobra would stack up against the best modern iron under comparable test conditions. With the late-breaking introduction of the new 450-horsepower Dodge Viper RT/10, we have the perfect chance to contrast old against new, and settle one of the most persistent arguments in all of automobilia: Who's fastest?

The 427 Cobra's mind-flattening performance is the product of big power in a small package. Unburdened by sissy comfort and safety frills, the Cobra weighs just 2480 pounds—a shocking 840 pounds less than the Viper. The low-tech 427-cubic-inch cast-iron Ford V-8 under the aluminum hood pounds out 485 gross horsepower at 6500. Gross measurement of horsepower makes for about 20 percent-higher numbers than the net measurement now commonly in use.

Both machines offer extremely high capabilities, but the Viper is the decisive victor from the driver's seat—if you're after composed control, not just stark excitement. A word never before applicable to the open Viper, the new RT/10s handling is virtually *viceless*, provided you know what you're doing. Drive the new version back to back with the earlier Viper and you'll discover that the suspension refinement lets you kick the tail out more effectively, and launch off the corners with even greater gusto—if such a thing is possible.

The Cobra is a challenge to drive, but the rewards are huge. Slewing half-side-ways though racetrack curves, sawing at the steering wheel while the sidepipes bellow, is an experience intense enough to make the hairs on the back of your neck stand on end for weeks afterwards.

Even with a slightly greasy starting area, the RT/10 hammered to 60 miles per hour in only 4.1 seconds—a half-second swifter than the bellowing Cobra. The quarter mile flashed by in an intense 12.3 seconds (the Cobra trailed by 0.4 second) with a terminal speed of 117.9 miles per hour (by then the Cobra was receding in the Dodge's mirrors at the rate of over 5 miles per hour). That's big-time acceleration!

Which brings us to the inevitable issue of 0-100-0 miles per hour accelerate/stop. That's a question the Viper RT/10 can answer in just 14.5 seconds—even on a comparatively slick surface. The Cobra 427 S/C needs an extra 1.1 seconds to make the trip. End of argument.

~*Motor Trend*, September 1997

New hardtop design didn't require removal of the black trim piece on the sport bar.

Blue with white stripes combo is the only time the RT/10 came with full stripes from the front spoiler to the rear fascia.

On U.S. cars, rear exit exhaust began in 1996 and continued through 2002. All Chrysler-imported European-spec cars came with rear exit exhaust.

New polished aluminum five-spoke rims.

RT/10 received most of the coupe's upgrades this year, including power windows, outside door handles, and a new interior with body-color accents on the steering wheel, shift knob, and handbrake. (This car has been fitted with an aftermarket shift knob and climate control knobs.)

New 450-horsepower engine.

One of three red 1997 RT/10s with tan interior and gold wheels.

Richard Fogg

1998 RT/10

Collectibility: **

Dodge completed the transition to the second generation for the RT/10 in 1998 by switching to the GTS-style hood with its NACA duct and vents and the deeper front chin spoiler. Both the GTS and RT/10 switched from cast-iron exhaust manifolds to tubular-type headers. Power window switches went from rocker switches to toggle-type switches. Next-generation air bags with lower force were added with a cut-off switch in case a child seat was used in the passenger seat.

Metallic silver (code PA9) was the new color for 1998, in addition to solid red. Black was the only interior color choice, now without any color accents.

Viper Specifications 1997–1998 RT/10	
Engine	8.0 L V-10
Bore/Stroke	4.00" x 3.88"
Power (bhp @ rpm)	450 @ 5200
Torque (lb-ft @ rpm*	490 @ 3700
Compression Ratio	9.6:1
Transmission	6-spd manual
Final Drive	3.07:1
Wheelbase	96.2"
Track (front/rear)	59.6"/60.6"
Overall Length	176.7"
Overall Width	75.7"
Overall Height	43.9"
Curb Weight	3319 lbs
Weight distribution	50/50
Ground Clearance	5.0"
Coefficient of Drag (cd)	0.495
Fuel Tank Capacity	19 gallons
Engine Oil	8 quarts
Frame	Tubular space frame
Front Suspension	Independent, unequal length A-arms
Front Shocks	Coil-over, low pressure gas Adjustable rebound
Front Anti-roll Bar	Tubular 27 mm diameter
Rear Suspension	Independent, unequal length A-arms
Rear shocks	Coil-over, low pressure gas Adjustable rebound
Rear Anti-roll bar	Tubular 22 mm diameter
Steering	Power rack & pinion
Front Brakes	13" vented discs with 4-piston calipers
Rear Brakes	13" vented discs with single piston calipers
Front Wheels	10" x 17" cast aluminum
Rear Wheels	13" x 17" cast aluminum
Front Tires	Michelin Pilot SX275/40 ZR17
Rear Tires	Michelin Pilot SX 335/35 ZR17
Tire pressure	29 psi

What They Said in 1998

Roadster production increased to 400 (in 1998), but build numbers remain solidly in favor of the coupe. In a way, that's too bad, because much of the Viper's pleasure derives from sensory experiences only available without a roof.

By up-rating the RT/10's motor from its original 400 horsepower to 450 horsepower, Dodge has made the RT/10 the snappiest Viper in the stable. Part is due to the fact that the roadster's throttle pedal is more responsive than the delay-action model in the coupe. And part is due to the fact Dodge imbued the suspension geometry of the coupe with more understeer than the roadster.

I came into this test thinking the roadster would be a dead dog in such vaunted Le Mans replica territory. Well, much to my surprise, it didn't work out that way at all.

~Sports Car International, Aug/Sept 1999

I Bought a 1998 Viper

Wondering how the first generation roadsters compare with the second generation? Jim Harley has had both. Here's what he thinks:

There I was, the 110-percent satisfied owner of one cool, fast, white 1996 Viper roadster—my dream car! With just 20,000 miles on the clock and a new pair of Michelins on the back, I wouldn't dare think of owning some other car! I had completely become accustomed to traveling light, and never seemed to mind having to pack the sliding Lexan side windows in the trunk when going for a drive around the track, or during my summer road trips through the state of Montana (to do a little "spirited" driving).

Then, in November of 1998, all that changed. My girlfriend Wendy suggested I look at the *new* roadsters. In a few short days it dawned on me that my car's standard warranty was almost up, the paint was thin, and its blue stripes were chipped. The Generation I Viper's stock cassette deck couldn't play my favorite CDs, and the speedo in my 415-horsepower car only went up to 180 miles per hour. I had, in fact, grown a little weary of having to scrub the black brake dust off of the 1996's white-painted alloy wheels.

The 1998 Gen II roadsters were gorgeous. They arrived fully improved with 450 big horses, dual air bags, doors that could actually be locked, and even outside door handles! The 200-watt CD player featured three automatic volume curves. The speedo topped out at 200 miles per hour. And, as a special bonus for 1998, Dodge was offering the new RT/10s in Viper Bright Metallic Silver for the first time! With the matching factory hardtop, polished alloy wheels, and a new seven-year Dodge warranty thrown in, it was no contest. I was absolutely SOLD!

Over the years, I am reminded of my good fortune in finding my silver RT/10. The power roll-up windows equate to total convenience, add to comfort, and indirectly, add more available trunk space. For a mere $75 large, the 1998 Viper roadster was—and, after 24,000 thrilling miles still is—an incomparable experience to own and drive. Total strangers remark, "Bond . . . James Bond," when I drive up. They've said, "You *must* be a movie star to drive a *beautiful* car like that!" Some have asked, "Did you win the lottery?!" And one lady exclaimed, "*What* an *amazing* car!" I am compelled to agree.

1998 RT/10 Chrysler

1998 Garage Watch

Under the hood, tubular exhaust headers.

GTS-style NACA duct and vents in hood.

1998 roadster received the GTSs front fascia with its deeper chin spoiler.

Lower-force air bags with cut-off switch.

Last year for fog lamp covers.

Corners of front spoiler are prone to scrapes.

Ron Kimball

1999 RT/10

Collectibility: ***

Despite many recent updates, even more improvements were made in 1999. According to Dodge literature, the new 18-inch five-spoke wheels came painted or polished, though I have only seen polished. Eighteen-inch Michelin Pilot Sport tires were also new. Team Viper finally succumbed to customer demands for power side mirrors. Inside, sun visors were switched from vinyl to cloth, the shift knob was switched to a golf-ball-shaped knob, and satin aluminum trim brightened up the door handles, shifter, and e-brake handle. A new reddish-brown Cognac leather interior was available as an option in addition to standard black.

Outside, fog light covers were deleted, and black (code PX3) was brought back to the color palette in addition to red and silver.

All these improvements make the 1999 RT/10 and later roadsters worth considering if you're planning to drive it on a regular basis.

Viper Specifications 1999–2002 RT/10	
Engine	8.0 L V-10
Bore/Stroke	4.00" x 3.88"
Power (bhp @ rpm)	450 @ 5200
Torque (lb-ft @ rpm*	490 @ 3700
Compression Ratio	9.6:1
Transmission	6-spd manual
Final Drive	3.07:1
Wheelbase	96.2"
Track (front/rear)	59.6"/60.6"
Overall Length	176.7"
Overall Width	75.7"
Overall Height	43.9"
Curb Weight	3319 lbs
Weight distribution	50/50
Ground Clearance	5.0"
Coefficient of Drag (cd)	0.495
Fuel Tank Capacity	19 gallons
Engine Oil	8 quarts
Frame	Tubular space frame
Front Suspension	Independent, unequal length A-arms
Front Shocks	Coil-over, low pressure gas Adjustable rebound
Front Anti-roll Bar	Tubular 27 mm diameter
Rear Suspension	Independent, unequal length A-arms
Rear shocks	Coil-over, low pressure gas Adjustable rebound
Rear Anti-roll bar	Tubular 22 mm diameter
Steering	Power rack & pinion
Front Brakes	13" vented discs with 4-piston calipers
Rear Brakes	13" vented discs with single piston calipers
Front Wheels	10" x 18" forged aluminum
Rear Wheels	13" x 18" forged aluminum
Front Tires	Michelin Pilot Sport 275/35 ZR18
Rear Tires	Michelin Pilot Sport 335/30 ZR18
Tire pressure	
Notes	2001-02 w/ABS

What They Said in 1999

You don't sit in a Viper; you wear it like a glove. The first five minutes in one is spent adjusting the seat, steering wheel, and pedal assembly to your liking. Yes, we said the pedal assembly.

The Viper is more car than 99.9 percent of the people driving them need. Its performance limits far exceed those of most drivers. That anyone actually needs to buy the go-fast add-ons available or send it for supertuning is laughable. It's like the difference between having $2 million in the bank or $10 million; At that point, your life doesn't change a bit—it's strictly a power trip. After spending the better part of four days and 1,400 miles in one, we'd recommend that every Viper owner attend a 3-day driving school and consider that your first bolt-on.

Other than that, all we can say is we want one—bad!

~*Mopar Muscle*, December 1999

I Bought a 1999 Viper

In addition to having owned a 1995, 1999, and 2003 Viper, Marco Chavez also owns a 1999 Corvette and 1998 Jaguar XK8. But the Viper is his favorite.

I love the way the Viper looks and the unbelievable amount of torque it has. A lot of cars are fun to drive, but the Viper is truly *exciting* to drive. I chose the 1999 Viper because it had roll-up windows, a little more horsepower, and it was a little more refined than my 1995 RT/10. Since I drive the car rain or shine about three times a week, it was very nice to be able to roll the windows up, though I must admit that I miss the sidepipes.

The brakes could be a little better. On really hard stopping, the right front brake tends to lock up. Also, the side sills get a little hot from the exhaust pipes, but it's a small price to pay for such a great car.

I've had only positive experiences with the car. Everyone is always very complimentary about the car. One of the most unbelievable experiences I've had was when I took the car on track at the Viper Owner's Invitational in Las Vegas. My adrenalin was still rushing an hour later. I will never forget that experience.

Even though I've owned Vipers for about seven years now, I still look forward to driving my car. The excitement, the experience, and the thrill are amazing. There are many great sport cars on the market, and I have been fortunate to have owned many of them, but after awhile, the thrill of the car usually wears out and it just becomes another nice car. This has not been the case with the Viper. After all these years, it is still something I look forward to driving every day. If you're thinking about buying a Viper, I can only say, don't wait—go buy one today so you can start having fun with a great car!

Power side mirrors.

No fog lamp covers.

New optional Cognac leather interior.

New golf-ball-style shift knob.

Interior received cloth sun visors and satin aluminum trim.

New 18-inch-diameter five-spoke wheels and Michelin Pilot Sport tires.

Chrysler

2000 RT/10

Collectibility: **

The 2000 model year saw a revised engine package (same power) to meet EPA requirements. This included a milder cam with 6 degrees less overlap; revised "high leakdown" lifters to smooth out idle; and lighter, stronger eutectic cast-aluminum pistons replacing the forged pistons.

The only other change was the addition of a metallic Steel Gray (code PS6) color, which replaced silver. Red and black continued to be available.

I Bought a 2000 Viper

Can a big guy fit in a Viper? Ask Cameron Corry. He's 6' 4" and weighs 290 lbs.

I first saw the Viper concept car at the 1990 auto show in San Francisco. It was love at first sight. It had that big wow factor. After that, every time I saw one on the street, it was "bat-turn" and follow it home so I could ask the owner all sorts of questions. I think I scared a few people doing that, being a big guy and all.

I've had muscle cars ever since I was old enough to drive. But after years of all those safe and sane cars of the '70s and '80s, I missed the "head-slamming-back-in-the-headrest" feeling. The Viper gives you that for as long as you hold the pedal down.

I chose a steel gray roadster because I loved the color, and it was available for only one year. It's not so dark as to obscure the lines, but not so bright that it would attract too much attention. I've lowered the seat so I can fit in the car, but it's still not a car I'd want to take on a long trip, but it's great for some fun back road blasts.

A friend took me for a ride around the race track in his Viper. I got hooked, so I started to race my RT/10, but my wife didn't want me hacking up that beautiful car to install all the safety equipment—so instead she encouraged me to buy a coupe. So now, I also have a 1996 blue with white stripes GTS for the track! The only problem with racing a Viper is the rising cost of replacement parts. My advice if you're going to race your Viper is to replace the hood and front fascia with cheaper aftermarket pieces so if they get damaged, it won't cost as much to fix.

Steel gray color makes a one year appearance. Red and black are also available.

What They Said in 2000

For this shootout of all shootouts, we've assembled America's three current air-sucking, fuel-mixing, spark-igniting, tire-melting, horsepower-producing champions. The limited-production 2000 SVT Cobra R . . . [the] new 2001 Z06 Corvette . . . [and] the 2000 Dodge Viper, [which] enters this fray to defend its title as kickass champ of American blacktop. But forget bench racing and lies. We don't guess: We test.

The Mustang beat the Corvette to 60 by 0.01 second with a 4.52 run. But the Cobra R gave back that edge by the end of the quarter, finishing 0.02 behind the Chevy with a 12.88/112.77 performance. At the end of 1320 feet, the Viper stands as the king of this hill: 4.25 seconds 0–60 and a 12.33/118.19 quarter is awesome in anybody's book.

The 0–100–0 contest pitted spectacular acceleration (matched with very good braking) against spectacular braking (matched with excellent acceleration). The spectacular acceleration/very good braking combo won, with the Viper beating the Vette 13.88 seconds to 14.17 seconds. The Cobra finished third at 14.91 seconds.

Our slalom test quantifies one of the many components of handling: stability in radical transitions. The Cobra R whipped out a blistering 69.3-miles per hour run, with the Viper just a whisker back at 69.2. The Corvette/Z06 was third with a still-impressive 68.4 miles per hour run.

~*Motor Trend*, August 2000

So now here we are in the year 2000—the New Millennium. And once again, the automotive gods have smiled upon this humble writer. DaimlerChrysler dropped off this shiny new Steel Gray Pearl Coat Viper RT/10 with the Connolly Leather Bucket Package.

Using what we've come to know as the best starting line technique for a Viper, I brought the tach to 1,500 rpm and waited for green. Then it was easy-out with the clutch and softly-on with the gas for about a car length and then, no holds barred. I power-shifted second gear and the car literally turned 90 degrees to the right in the blink of an eye—at full second gear throttle. It was the scariest moment I've ever had in an automobile.

Several runs were made in the 12.0 range with launch technique and shift rpm varied slightly . . . but I wanted more. I wanted an 11-second time slip. Halfway down the track I kept telling myself, "This isn't going to be a good run—it just feels slow." But the timeslip said 11.97/115.57. YES! The 2000 Viper RT/10 had eclipsed the magical 11 second barrier and was now the new record holder.

~*High Performance Mopar*, October 2000

Revised engine to meet EPA requirements.

Maurice Q. Liang

2001 RT/10

Collectibility: ✶✶✶✶

The big news for 2001 was the addition of the ABS. Gen II Vipers had a tendency to lock up the wheels (usually the right front) under heavy braking such as panic stops and in autocross situations. This was likely due to the right front corner having about 80 pounds less riding on it. ABS solved this problem. Retrofitting an older Viper with ABS is cost-prohibitive, so if you plan to take your Viper to the track, it's worth considering 2001 and newer.

A one-year-only deep metallic Sapphire Blue (code PBW) replaced Steel Gray. Yellow was brought back, having been gone since 1995. This time, it was a brighter yellow called "Viper Race Yellow" (code PYR). Red, of course, continued to be available. Customers continued to have a choice of a black or optional Cognac interior.

2001 car continued using the wide spoke design.

I Bought a 2001 Viper

Dennis and Tracy Kimball own a beautiful sapphire blue RT/10:

I had always thought about owning a Viper, so when it became practical, I started thinking about buying a used one on the Internet. But when I learned that the 2001 Viper was going to have ABS, I changed my mind and decided to buy a new one.

The last time I had a convertible was when I was in high school 30 years ago, and I had a dune buggy. I remember having great times in the California weather driving that car. So if I was going to pick a new car, it had to be convertible, which is why I chose the RT/10. And with its detachable hardtop, the RT/10 can seem like a coupe also, so you can have the best of both worlds.

The Viper is the kind of car that makes you look for excuses to drive it. I drive it to go get coffee, groceries, you name it. I did not buy this car as an investment to sit in the garage. Every time I get on the accelerator it makes my heart beat jump.

I love the sapphire blue color and the way it draws attention. The only drawback isthat it's hard to maintain. It shows every little flaw.

I bought the car because it always had a mystique to it. What I did not realize until after buying the car was how much fun the car *club* would be. The people in the Viper Club are all so nice and easy going. You fit right in regardless of your social standing.

One of my most memorable events was going to Nashville for the Viper Owners Invitational. That was amazing to see 800 Vipers and 1,600 people all in the same place.

My advice? What are you waiting for? It is more than just a car, it is a ticket into a great car club—one of the best in the world!

New sapphire color makes a one-year appearance.

New ABS.

Aftermarket side vent covers.

The interior was updated in 1999 to include aluminum trim and golf-ball-style shift knob.

Maurice Q. Liang

2002 RT/10

Collectibility: ****

Two thousand two was the final year for the original-style Viper RT/10, which makes it more collectible. The 2001 and 2002 are also the best all-around RT/10s for daily use. A one-year Graphite Metallic (code PDR) replaced Sapphire, while red and yellow continued to be available.

I Bought a 2002 Viper

Jon Luhmann got one of the final year roadsters:

My Viper was a surprise birthday gift—a graphite metallic RT/10. I like the Viper's great blend of style and muscle, and the fact that I can have the choice of a hard-top or a soft top. I've owned several older-model Corvettes and muscle cars, but the Viper's been the most fun car to date.

In the two years I've owned it, I've only had two problems. One was a torn window weather stripping, and the other was a sticky door button.

Along with the Viper came good times and a new group of friends in the Viper club. Driving it is exhilarating and puts a smile on my face. Every time I drive my Viper down the coast or in the mountains with the top down, I experience moments where life seems just too good to be true

Comparing Steel Gray (right) and Graphite RT/10s (left).

2002 Garage Watch

For final year of production of the original RT/10, there were no changes other than color. Graphic metallic (shown) made a one year appearance. Red and yellow continued to be available.

Maurice Q. Liang

The second generation of Vipers began in 1996 with the new GTS coupes. 1999 silver ACR, 1998 white GT2, red and blue standard GTSs.

Chapter 4

1996–2002 GTS Coupes

In 1996, Dodge introduced the Viper GTS coupe, with its fixed, double-bubble roof, fast-back glass hatch, and duck-tail spoiler. The GTS is much more than just an RT/10 with new body panels. Team Viper took advantage of the re-design to address some of the shortcomings of the earlier cars. They took weight out of the chassis and re-designed the V-10 engine to improve cooling, reduce weight, and increase power, while retaining the same displacement.

Because it was a coupe, the Viper now had to have roll-up windows. To make room for the window assembly, the seat-belt retracting mechanisms were moved from the door to the in-board side of the seats. Electrically-operated outside door handles were also added, as there was no room for traditional mechanical rods.

Inside, the coupe received an all-new, all-black interior. The dash featured bumps over the center gauges, and the tach and speedometer, increased to 200 miles per hour, swapped locations. The climate control module and the stereo (now an in-dash CD player) also swapped locations to allow room behind the dash for the air bag controller. Dual air bags were standard. The driver's air bag was located in a new steering wheel design. Since the passenger air bag took up the space where the old glove box was located, a small glove box and a netted storage compartment were added behind the center console where the woofers resided in the roadster. The woofers were moved to the back of the trunk area. Though still nowhere as good as an aftermarket system, the new stereo sounded better than the old one. The Alpine head unit featured a selectable 3-level automatic volume control that would adjust the volume based upon the speed of the car.

New seats made by Johnson Controls replaced the Lear seats from the roadster and featured a perforated, breathable leather. Also new was the industry's first manually-adjustable pedal cluster, making it easier for short drivers to reach the pedals. Overhead were two adjustable map lights and a netted pocket. Power window switches were placed where the fog light switches previously resided on the center console. Fog lights were now activated by pulling on the headlamp switch, which was now a rotating knob.

The Chrysler corporate ignition key, used on previous Vipers, was finally replaced with a key specific to the Viper that featured the snake emblem as the key head.

Being a more "useable" car, Dodge engineers dialed in some understeer to take the Viper off its knife-edge handling at the limit. The new suspension, settings, and tires also made the handling less darty, improved wet weather traction, and gave the GTS a more supple ride.

To reduce the jerking motion that happened when the large throttle bodies first cracked open at slow speeds, engineers programmed a slight delay in the engine control unit when the throttle was suddenly closed and used a mechanical linkage between the two throttle bodies.

Dodge offered a voucher program to reward loyal Viper owners. If you were the original owner of an RT/10 and still owned it, you received a voucher that would allow you to place an order for a first-year coupe. Dealers could not order a first-year GTS without this voucher. Consequently, about 75% of the first year of production was sold to current Viper owners. A limited run of RT/10 roadsters was produced before GTS production began slowly in the Spring of 1996.

Over the years, Dodge continued to improve the GTS, but always keeping in mind the pure-performance mantra. Some of the major GTS milestones include the highly desirable blue with white stripes color combination available only in 1996 and 1997, the limited-edition 1998 GT2, a number of improvements for 1999, the ACR club racer option introduced in 1999, and the addition of ABS in 2001.

1996 GTS Coupe

Collectibility: ****

The all-new 1996 GTS debuted in one color combination: blue (code PBE) with white stripes (code# QW1). This color combination is *the* classic color combination, making this the most collectible color combination of the coupes. This was the only year/model Viper that was *not* available in red.

Compared with the concept car, the production version had a less pronounced chin spoiler, rear-exit exhausts instead of side pipes, and a Viper emblem center high-mount stop light (CHMSL) instead of a strip of LEDs.

The new five-spoke wheels were made of cast-aluminum, but because of their porous surface, were difficult to polish to a high shine. The shortage of wheels held up release of the GTS for several months. It was not unusual to see GTSs stored at the plant sitting on space-saver tires.

Since the 1996 GTS was a first-year car, there are some inevitable things to look for. Many, but not all, 1996 and even some 1997 coupes leak water at the top of the windshield near the rearview mirror during heavy rains. This was due to a gap in the sealant where one side met the other.

It's not uncommon for 1996 GTSs to leak oil from the rear main seal cover gasket. Look for oil dripping from the bottom of the car just under where the base of the windshield meets the hood. Fortunately, this is not a major repair. They are also prone to leaking from the timing cover gasket in front of the engine. Again, not a major repair.

Some engines that consumed abnormal amounts of oil were discovered to be missing the valve stem seals on one side of the engine. This is a more major repair, but most likely, any cars with this problem have already been repaired.

A common complaint was a rattling sound heard when the coupe was left in neutral, clutch pedal out, with the engine idling. This was called "neutral gear rattle" and was caused by the unloaded gears vibrating from the lopey engine idle. It's not a problem, but if it bothers you, the recommended solution was to replace the transmission fluid with thicker fluid.

Another complaint was driveline clunk. A mistake with the supplier resulted in the axle shaft splines being cut straight instead of with a 1-degree twist. When the driveline loaded up, it would produce a clunk sound. It's not a problem that hurts the car.

Early GTSs were prone to breaking off the rubber molding at the top rear of the door glass. The problem was later solved by replacing the door glass with one that had a more rounded corner.

Manufacturing the GTSs glass hatch with no external bumps or bolt heads was quite an engineering feat. Occasionally, the glue used to hold the latch to the glass would let go on early GTSs. The best way to prevent this is to not slam the glass hatch when closing it. Just push it firmly until it latches. Also, the gas struts that push the glass hatch up wear out over time and no longer support the glass. These are easily replaceable.

Another common problem is corrosion on the aluminum gas cap cover. The two different metals between the housing and the pins caused corrosion along the hinge.

A final little detail—early 1996 GTSs did not come with the clear plastic protector tape on the lower corners of the front spoiler. These were added in mid-production.

Viper Specifications 1996–1998 GTS	
Engine	8.0 L V-10
Bore/Stroke	4.00" x 3.88"
Power (bhp @ rpm)	450 @ 5200
Torque (lb-ft @ rpm*	490 @ 3700
Compression Ratio	9.6:1
Transmission	6-spd manual
Final Drive	3.07:1
Wheelbase	96.2"
Track (front/rear)	59.6"/60.6"
Overall Length	176.7"
Overall Width	75.7"
Overall Height	47.0"
Curb Weight	3375 lbs
Weight distribution	46/54
Ground Clearance	5.0"
Coefficient of Drag (cd)	0.35
Fuel Tank Capacity	19 gallons
Engine Oil	8 quarts
Frame	Tubular space frame
Front Suspension	Independent, unequal length A-arms
Front Shocks	Coil-over, low pressure gas Adjustable rebound
Front Anti-roll Bar	Tubular 27 mm diameter
Rear Suspension	Independent, unequal length A-arms
Rear shocks	Coil-over, low pressure gas Adjustable rebound
Rear Anti-roll bar	Tubular 22 mm diameter
Steering	Power rack & pinion
Front Brakes	13" vented discs with 4-piston calipers
Rear Brakes	13" vented discs with single piston calipers
Front Wheels	10" x 17" cast aluminum*
Rear Wheels	13" x 17" cast aluminum*
Front Tires	Michelin Pilot SX275/40 ZR17
Rear Tires	Michelin Pilot SX 335/35 ZR17
Tire pressure	29 psi
Notes	*forged aluminum in 1997 1-piece BBS on GT2

I Bought a 1996 Viper

Author Maurice Q. Liang was Founder and first National President of the Viper Club of America when the GTS coupe was introduced. Naturally, he had to have one.

I hadn't planned on buying a second Viper in three years. In fact, I thought I might buy a Camaro Z-28 as a daily driver for those days when it just wasn't practical to drive the roadster—80 percent of the bang for about 20 percent of the buck. But once I saw the GTS, it was love at first sight—again. They had captured lightning in a bottle a second time. The same, yet different. I knew I had to have it. It was a $70,000 Viper hardtop that came with a free Viper.

To reward loyal Viper owners, Dodge handed out vouchers for ordering the GTS at the 1995 Viper Owner's Invitational in Monterey. As soon as I had my voucher, I literally dragged my dealer, Phil Eiselin, out of the shower so we could FedEx the voucher back to Dodge in Detroit.

Ron Smith, Viper Marketing Manager at the time, scheduled the VCA president's cars to be built as the first customer cars. Not only was he rewarding us for our work in building the club, he knew we would be the least likely to complain if anything went wrong with the early cars!

Once they were built, he turned us loose in the plant's storage room. Picture a huge room filled to the brim with shiny new blue with white stripes GTSs waiting to be delivered. "Find the one with your name on it," he said. Like kids in a candy shop, we ran through the room looking for our names and calling to others when we found theirs. It was a magical moment.

As weird as this sounds, when I ordered my coupe, I wondered if it might be just a bit boring. "How different could it be from the roadster?" I thought. A lot, as it turns out. The roadster is my sunny day, wind-in-your-face amusement park ride. A very visceral experience. I love it. It's my favorite car of all time. But the coupe lets me have the power and the handling of the Viper when I don't want such a visceral experience. Like when it's cold. Or when I have a date in the city. Or at the track. Oh the track. Even going up the steep hill on the back side of Laguna Seca Raceway, the GTS pulls like a freight train—for as long as you dare hold your foot down. It's incredible. And the cornering forces can make your head go light.

These 1996 Viper GTSs sat on space-saver tires waiting for the new polished five-spoke wheels before they could be shipped from the factory.

Bob Lutz piloted the 1996 GTS as the pace car for Indy. Replica decal sets were available separately from Dodge.

What They Said in 1996

For the GTS coupe, Team Viper executive engineer Roy Sjoberg says there were five goals. Reduce weight. Improve weight distribution (more weight on the rear tires). Improve aerodynamics. Improve power and performance. And finally, meet 1997 safety standards.

"We liked the roadster," he says, "but some people want more refinement." We'll say. Sjoberg went on to add that this Viper would be "more of a grand-touring car."

Despite the visual similarity between the 1996 RT/10 roadster and the GTS coupe, the two share few body pieces—just the door skins and the side sills. The result, though, is a stunner.

The GTS blasts out of the hole to 60 miles per hour in four seconds flat, past 100 miles per hour in 9.2 seconds, and through the quarter-mile in 12.3 seconds at 115 miles per hour. But just what do those numbers *feel* like? This kind of thrust renders your passenger momentarily speechless. It makes your radar detector take flying death leaps off the sun visor toward your forehead. The GTS coupe, in fact, will overtake every U.S.-legal production car we've tested this side of the now-defunct Ferrari F40 and Lamborghini Diablo.

But the GTS coupe is much more than 8.0 liters of V-10 stoked on an equal amount of espresso. Handling-wise, the Dodge boys managed to excise most of the Viper's nasty traits while somehow maintaining its quick reflexes. The sensitive but nervous steering that required an extremely smooth hand is now even-tempered and is no longer distracted by imperfect pavement. Despite its huge rubber (more rubber, in fact, than on any other production car for sale in the United States), the coupe maintains an acceptable ride. Bump harshness is minimal, although the chassis can still get flustered over really rough pavement.

To appreciate the GTS, you'll want to head for the track, where it works marvelously. Chrysler let us unwind the new coupe at the famous Nurburgring racetrack in Germany. Much like the Nurburgring-bred Porsche 911, the GTS coupe seems to work better the faster you go. The chassis rewards proper technique and smooth inputs with astonishingly fast corner velocities, and the Brembo brakes, sans ABS, bring it down reliably. Even on the track, the power borders on the absurd: The GTS tackled the 'Ring's uphill climb before the Karussell with such ferocity that our passenger, European correspondent Peter Robinson, and I (behind the wheel) could only chuckle in amazement.

If Team Viper's sixth goal was for the GTS to make the exotic-car history books, it can rest easy. Performance on bulging bodywork like this is nothing if not exotic.

~*Car and Driver*, September 1996

I prefer to put every second of free time into rollicking, on-the-edge, nobody-will-believe-this use. In other words, I play too hard. My passion, as I've admitted before in the pages of *FORTUNE*, is cars.

Why the Viper Coupe?

When I came down to the [hotel] lobby, the place was empty—the entire staff was on the sidewalk, trying to figure out what the car was and whether it would bite if approached too closely. In fairness, I took a big step back myself: This muscly, low-slung, swoopy rocket was unlike anything else I'd seen on the street. I slid into the luscious black leather wraparound driver's seat, turned the key, and smiled at the deep-throated sound of all ten cylinders growling to life.

At first, tooling around town, I was distracted by the Viper's long-traveling clutch, serious white-on-black instrumentation, and hulking presence. I was also distracted because people stared, hitchhiked, drag-raced, and, in one man's case, video-taped the Viper—while he was driving. It was time to find empty, snaking roads.

Turning off the CD player so I could better focus on the James Earl Jones bass of the engine, I dropped into first gear and floored it. The Viper whiplashed me into the seatback and shot into a sweeping corner—powerful, graceful, game for anything. To its credit, it has the smoothness of a grand touring car, but its soul is a wild thing, arrogant and assured in every move, barely tamed by my puny attempts at control.

I had fallen in love—not a tender, sweet love, but the searing, blood-pounding kind. This is a car for people who live by extremes and never choose the middle road. I'll be calling a dealer shortly. As I headed to the hotel, a crazed pit bull hanging out the back of a station wagon caught sight of the Viper and began barking hysterically. It takes one to know one.

~Sue Zesiger, *FORTUNE*, September 30, 1996

Indy Pace Car

The GTS served as the Indy Pace Car in 1996, with Bob Lutz as the driver. Aside from the strobe lights and the sunroof, the real Indy Pace Car was no different from a production Viper. Dodge sold 100 of the Indy Pace Car decal sets separately; none left the factory with the decals in or on the car. Initially, not all the decal sets sold, so they were later closed out on sale. Amazingly, collectors are only now discovering the value of these decals. A limited-edition matching blue with white strips Ram pickup was also produced.

1996 Garage Watch

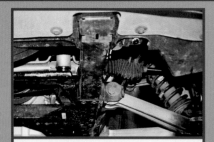

Triangular reinforcement were added to the frame rails to strengthen the steering rack and frame as part of a recall on 1996-1999 GTSs.

New Viper-head ignition key (right) replaced the Chrysler corporate key.

Roll-up windows added weight to doors, which tend to sag over time and require readjustment. Check for rubbing and worn weather stripping.

New in-dash AM/FM/CD player, six-speaker stereo. New dash and center console.

New 450-horsepower engine.

NACA duct and vents in hood.

It's not unusual to find autographs on Vipers from plant craftspersons, as many original owners requested them to sign the cars. This spare tire cover was painted and autographed by Team Viper members.

Gas caps tend to corrode near the hinge.

Stripes run through the license plate area (red pinstripe is owner-added) on 96 cars.

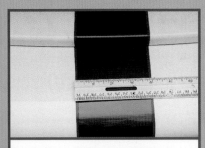

Stripes in rear license area (8.25 inches wide, 4-inch space between). Red pin stripe is owner-added.

Outside door handles and drop glass.

Gas struts used to raise the glass hatch wear out over time and must be replaced.

Two-piece window trim tends to lift.

Cast-aluminum five-spoke wheels, polished and clear coated.

Rear exit exhaust.

Ron Kimball

1997 GTS

Collectibility: ****

The 1997 GTS was mostly a continuation of production for the recently introduced 1996 GTS coupe. To fill the backlog of orders, Dodge continued building the blue with white stripes paint scheme for another year, with a few minor changes. To make it easier for the factory to paint, the white stripes are slightly narrower on the 1997 car (8 inches wide instead of 8 1/4 inches), resulting in a wider blue space between the stripes (4 7/16 inches versus 4 inches). Also, the easiest way to tell a 1997 blue with white stripes GTS from a 1996 is to look at the rear license plate area. On the 1996 cars, the stripes run through the license plate indent. On the 1997 cars, the stripes skip past the indent.

Red was also added to the palette for the GTS in 1997. Optionally with red cars, customers could order the yellow wheel package or the sparkle gold wheel package.

The cast-aluminum five-spoke wheels were replaced with forged wheels. The easiest way to tell the difference is to look for a weld bead around the rim behind the face on the cast wheels. The forged wheels don't have this bead. The other difference is that the forged wheels are shinier, because the surface is less porous.

Inside, an unattractive but legally necessary bright yellow air bag label was stamped into the sun visor. Underneath, the Dana 44 rear end was replaced with a Dana Super 44, which had thicker bolts.

I Bought a 1997 Viper

Terri Angen is not only one of the rare women that own a Viper—she owns two—a 1996 RT/10 and a 1997 GTS.

I had wanted a red sports car my whole life. I fell in love with the Viper in 1989 when I saw it at a car show. In 1996, my husband Rocky surprised me with a black 1996 RT/10. Then, in 1997 I was having my RT/10 serviced at the dealership. Dodge had just come out with a red GTS coupe, and there happened to be one on the showroom floor. We went to look at it, and I fell in love with it. This was my red dream car! My wonderful husband insisted I needed a winter car (since my black Viper is a roadster) and before I knew it, I was driving this beautiful red GTS coupe off the showroom floor.

I love the looks. I definitely love the power—smooth. . . fast . . . secure. I love how excited people get when they see it! The Viper seems to always bring a smile to everyone's face . . . young and old. I love how special Dodge makes Viper owners feel, especially with the Viper Owners Invitationals. How cool is it to be someplace with a thousand Vipers?

The quirks are minor—the interior squeaks, the neutral gear rattle, the A/C loses its charge every so often, and the doors lock when the battery goes dead. But I love the car so much that I'd live with quirks even if they were major!

Owning a Viper compares to nothing I have ever done. I'll never forget the first day I had it. I went through a full tank of gas just giving rides to all my son's friends. We have met so many truly amazing people, all brought together because of our love for the Viper. I have to say . . . we are definitely a fun group of car enthusiasts!

Being a woman-owner is a little different. I remember the first time a man looked in my roadster and said to my husband "Hey! How come you're letting her drive?" And Rocky's reply was, "because it's *her* car!"

Don't think about it . . . just do it! I promise you won't be sorry. It will be the most positive, fun experience of your life! I still get a big smile on my face each and every time I jump in one of my Vipers!

What They Said in 1997

Few legends truly live up to their press. The Dodge Viper GTS, on the other hand, exceeds the hyperbole that engulfs it. The Dodge people claim a 490-pound-foot wallop out of the 8.0-liter V-10; believe them. In a car that weighs just 68 pounds more than the diminutive Porsche 911 Turbo, this torque translates into immediate, brutal—almost terrifying—throttle response. Mercifully, the GTS has a better composed, far more predictable chassis than that of the original RT/10. But it's still pure, unvarnished, wet-your-pants performance.

The GTS cut a swath of destruction through our ten tests, winning six of them outright, and only faltering significantly in 60-0 miles per hour braking and on the wet skidpad. Although it only required 4.0 seconds for the 0-60-miles per hour challenge, the Viper couldn't match the Porsche's initial pounce off the line (and 3.7 second 0-60 performance); the GTS however, was the leader in the quarter mile, with a 12.2 second, 119.3-miles per hour pass, and then blew through the one-mile mark at 169.4 miles per hour (6.8 miles per hour faster than the 911), on its way to an atmosphere-battering terminal velocity of 187.3 miles per hour—5.5 miles per hour faster than the Black Forest bomber. A maximum lateral g reading of 1.01 on the dry skidpad combined with the GTSs unerring chassis response to allow a breathtaking production-record 73.6-miles per hour slalom pass; this tells you plenty about the way the Viper works. A pole position lap time on the road course tells you the rest—this is more race car than street car . . . There is simply no other production car like the wholly brutal Viper GTS.

~Motor Trend, May 1997

The Americans have always chuckled into their Buds about the namby-pamby way we Europeans tune our cars. While we fret about remapping microprocessors and reprofiling air intakes, their philosophy is much simpler: 'there ain't no substitute for cubes'. Ask a Yank to make a car go faster and he cranes a bigger engine into it. Period.

The real problem, though, is that our little island is just too small for the larger-than-life Viper to cope with—our roads are simply not wide enough. Sitting low down and in the left-hand side of the cockpit, you feel like a seven-year-old at the wheel of dad's car. Excited but kind of scared. Stiff suspension and monstrous tires also mean that every camber change, cats' eye, pothole or discarded matchstick has the car weaving away from your planned course.

The matte grey dash and trim look hard and cheap, the car reeks of that polyurethane glue they use in glass-fibre cars—you know, the stuff that smells like cat's pee—and the toys are limited to power windows, air-conditioning, and a 200-watt CD system.

The Viper GTS is sexier-looking than a [room] full of super-models and has an engine that makes Mike Tyson look puny, but if you really want to enjoy it you need to live in Montana—or have your own private airfield and large supply of tires.

~Top Gear, July 1997

Gold (shown) or yellow wheels were optional on the red cars in 1997.

Solid red (with no stripes) was added to the color choices in addition to the blue with white stripes.

Air conditioning hose connector tends to leak. A service bulletin was issued for repairs.

Air bag label was stamped into the sun visor in 1997.

1997 blue with white stripe cars had narrower stripes (8 inches) than the 1996 cars, and the stripes no longer passed through the rear license area.

New Dana Super 44 rear end.

Forged aluminum wheels were shinier than the 1996 cast-aluminum wheels.

Ron Kimball

1998 GTS

Collectibility: ** for regular GTS
***** for GT2

For 1998, Dodge switched from the heavier cast-iron headers to lighter, tubular-style exhaust headers. An air bag cutoff switch was added to allow owners to fit child seats in the passenger seat. Next-generation, lower-power air bags were also used.

Red continued in the color palette, and metallic silver (code PA9) replaced the blue with white stripes paint scheme as the other color choice. Red cars could be ordered with optional dual silver stripes (code QA9) while silver GTSs could be ordered with optional dual blue stripes (code QBE). The body-colored interior accents and the yellow and gold wheel/trim options were no longer available.

The big news for 1998 was the announcement of the factory-built special edition GT2. To commemorate their 1997 FIA GT2 manufacturer and driver championships, Dodge built 100 street-legal replicas of the Viper GTS/R race car. Based on a standard GTS, all GT2s were

What They Said in 1998

Most commemorative models are just sticker and badge jobs. But the Viper GTS/R (GT2) offers a bit more than only graphics. It wears the same kind of aerodynamic pieces as the original GTS/R. And Project Manager John Fernandez performed a few hot-rod tricks on the engine's induction system to make the car the most potent street-going Viper yet.

The rear wing is patterned after the one that appeared on the original GTS/R while the front splitter and winglets are from the first year's development of the car. But, according to Fernandez, they're the real thing—Chrysler even had the parts fabricated by the original suppliers. The only difference is that the rear wing is set at zero angle of incidence and can't be adjusted like the ones on the race cars.

The car, even in white, looks more menacing than the stock GTS, thanks to the flying airfoil and aggressive front splitter. One problem with owning a white Viper is that the heat from the exhaust pipes, which are still routed through the car's rocker panels before returning inboard to exit the rear, causes some discoloring on the exposed part of the doorsill.

The intake tubes were straightened, the airbox revised, and low-restriction K&N filters replace the stock units. These changes bumped the horsepower by 10 to 460 brake horsepower delivered at 5200 rpm. Better still, torque is now 500 lb-ft (up 10) and peaks 100 revs sooner at 3600 rpm.

The extra muscle showed at the drag strip where the GTS/R (GT2) blistered its way to 60 miles per hour in 4.2 seconds, a tenth quicker than our previous best with a standard GTS coupe. The car also showed improvement in the quarter-mile, recording a time of 12.5 sec., same as the GTS coupe, but with a higher trap speed of 118.5 miles per hour.

The GTS/R (GT2) further enhances the Viper's reputation as our hemisphere's king of performance numbers—it remains the quickest, best-handling sports car available from an American manufacturer.

~*Road & Track*, September 1998

Even though there's no change to the engine's internals or exhaust, you can hear the difference the new intake plumbing makes. As Senior Road Test Editor Mac DeMere snap-shifted the GT2 through our bevy of acceleration tests, it spoke in a deep, reedy howl like that of no other Viper. The new hardware must help a bit, too, as this white lightning rod turned in the fastest acceleration numbers (0–60 miles per hour in 4.0 seconds) we've ever recorded for a stock Viper.

There's an even more noticeable handling improvement via the lower-profile rolling stock. Braking feel and pedal modulation with the still-non-existent ABS discs were also the best of any Viper we've driven, and we've driven a bunch. Handling is sharper, crisper, and the limit of adhesion is higher—though once past that limit, rear-end breakaway is more dramatic.

There are three major problems with the $85,200 way-too-limited edition Viper GT2: 1) we had to give ours back, 2) Dodge only built 100 of them, 3) they're all sold.

~*Motor Trend*, April 1999

painted white with blue stripes like the race car and featured a large wing on the back, carbon-fiber air-splitters and side sills ground effects, and little winglets in the front. A foretelling of things to come, one-piece 18-inch BBS lace wheels in painted silver were used along with 18-inch Michelin Pilot MXX3 tires. These wheels appeared the following year as part of the ACR option.

Inside, the interior featured blue accent trim on the seats, center console, and door panels, red five-point harnesses with the ORECA race team labels (original three-point belts were also installed), and a dash plaque with the serial number of the car. The only changes under the hood were K&N free-flow air filters and smooth tubes to replace the corrugated stock intake tubes. The GT2 was rated at 460 horsepower and 500 lb-ft of torque.

GT2s came with a special car cover (shipped separately) to fit over the large wing, and each car had a disposable camera with undeveloped film capturing the assembly of the car. MSRP for the GT2 was $85,200, about $15,000 more than a standard GTS.

The GT2s are probably the most collectible street Vipers. Restoring one could be a difficult challenge, since the unique parts to the GT2 are no longer available, so it's best to buy one that is complete. The VINs on GT2s run in sequence, from 0 to 100.

I Bought a 1998 Viper

Steve Kingshott is a serious Viperholic. Not only does he own a 1998 GT2, a 1994 red RT/10, a 2001 red with silver stripes GTS, and a 2001 red with white stripes #91 Daytona replica, but he lives in the United Kingdom, which makes it even more challenging to own Vipers with the import requirements and the narrow roads.

U.K. import regulations are a nightmare. Imported cars have to be checked and approved for U.K. road use. For my #91 Daytona replica, the authorities made me remove the tow hook, rear wing, and windscreen sticker; move the passenger door mirror; change the handbrake cable position; change the exhaust; add side-repeating indicators and fog lights at the rear (onto the air diffuser); and a lot, lot more. All this took six to seven weeks after the car arrived and cost about U.S. $3,000 on top of the $4,000 shipping and insurance and the $20,000 import duty and tax!

Buying an officially imported one isn't simple, either. There are only around 60 Vipers in the whole of four countries that make up the U.K. It took me three months to find a car—a stunning red with silver stripes GTS that had been a Chrysler press car. Having found a car, then I had to shop around for insurance, as many companies will not insure them. Those that do usually specify a top alarm system (Thatcham Category 1), which means changing the standard one and sometimes adding a satellite tracker system as well. European-export Vipers come with the speedometer marked in kilometers, not miles. But here in the U.K., we still count in miles, so we have to convert the speedometer back to read miles.

Driving a Viper in the U.K. is a challenge as well. It's not unusual to find country roads that are only 8 to 10 feet wide—for *two-way* traffic! Even our motorways [freeways] are meant for small to medium-size U.K. vehicles. And parking—at any supermarket car park, it's not unusual to come back to find cars parked on either side of you with only an 18 inch space between them, so you cannot get into your car!

Filling up at the petrol [gas] station is a 30-minute affair. You stop, and by the time you exit the car, there is a crowd. You explain, raise the hood, fill with petrol, explain, lower the hood, explain, and go to pay. Five minutes explaining to the people waiting to pay, and you go back to—you guessed it—explain, raise the hood, explain . . . Ferraris and Lambos are common. Vipers are rare. Outside of Viper club events, I have seen fewer than 10 Vipers on the road in the last 12 years.

Owning a Viper is impractical, illogical, and absolutely special. Vipers to me are about passion and love. Why else would I do this? I love the "in your face" attitude, the raw power, the styling, and the general insanity. Boy racers, Ferraris, Suburus challenge and you do not respond. You know you are quicker. You know your car is special. You know—and they know.

1 of 100 special edition GT2s produced in 1998.

All 1998 GTSs received improved one-piece window trim.

Color accented interior with ORECA 5-point harnesses and dash plaque.

Last year to use fog light covers on all Vipers.

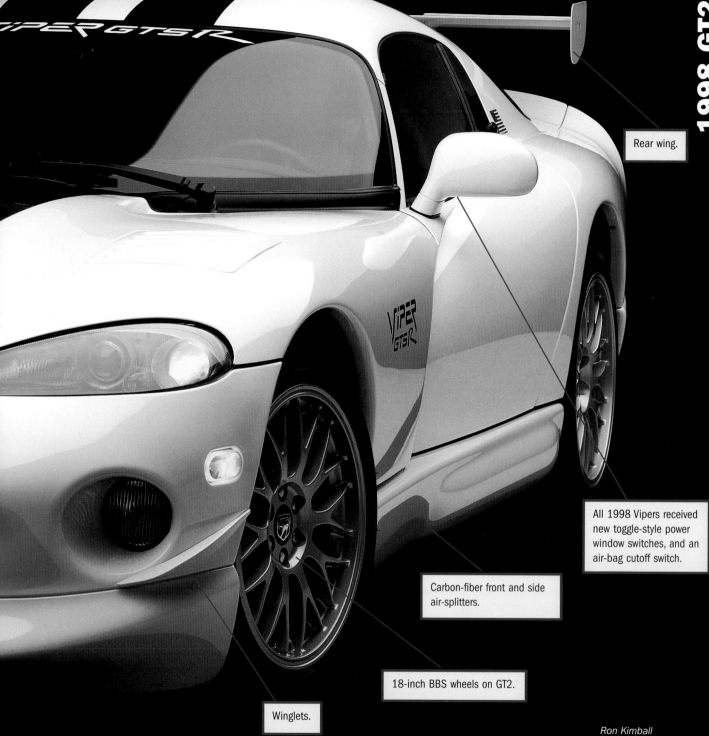

Rear wing.

All 1998 Vipers received new toggle-style power window switches, and an air-bag cutoff switch.

Carbon-fiber front and side air-splitters.

18-inch BBS wheels on GT2.

Winglets.

Ron Kimball

1999 GTS

Collectibility: ✱✱✱

Model year 1999 saw a number of refinements made to the Viper. A revised interior featured aluminum accents on the door handle, shift stalk, and e-brake handle. The taller gear-shift shaft was topped with a round, golf-ball-style shift knob. Power mirrors and a remote hatch release were also added. Sun visors were changed from vinyl to a fuzzy cloth. And an optional Connelly leather interior was available in a "Cognac" color.

Outside, the Viper no longer had the clear covers over the fog lights and sported new polished 18-inch five-spoke wheels with a smooth face and wider spokes. New Michelin Pilot Sports replaced the MXX3 tires, now in size 275/35 ZR 18 for the front and 335/30 ZR 18 for the rears.

Red and silver continued on, and solid black (code PX3) returned to the Viper's color palette. Red and black GTSs could be ordered with optional dual silver stripes (code QA9), while the silver GTS could be ordered with optional dual blue stripes (code QBE).

The exciting news for 1999 was the addition of the ACR option. Available only on the GTS, it was developed in response to the VCA members' request for a Viper designed for weekend racing (e.g., add performance parts, delete luxury equipment). For an additional $10,000, the ACR came with Koni adjustable shocks, Meritor heavy-duty springs, smooth air-intake hoses, K&N air filters, 18-inch BBS wheels, and five-point harnesses. The latter four made their debut on the limited-edition 1998 GT2. With the ACR package, the air conditioning, radio, and fog lamps were deleted to save weight, and optionally, ducts could be fitted to the fog lamp openings to feed air to the brakes. Although ACRs came standard with the radio and A/C deleted, most ACRs were ordered with an option that added back the radio and A/C (at extra cost, of course).

Mopar Parts also created additional race parts that could be added by the owner, which included a differential cooler, high-g-force oil pan, racing exhaust, and a lower final drive.

The stiffer ACR suspension, designed for the race track, gives the ACR a more "jiggly" ride, even on the softest setting. The car tends to ride over bumps, rather than absorb them. The challenge with adjustable suspensions is setting them up properly, which usually requires a lot of trial and error at a track. For street driving, a standard GTS offers a more comfortable ride.

Many ACRs were purchased for racing, so when buying a used one look for signs of modifications or abuse. Racers tend to drive their cars pretty hard and modify whatever it takes to improve their lap times, with little or no thought to maintaining originality.

Viper Specifications 1999–2002 GTS	
Engine	8.0 L V-10
Bore/Stroke	4.00" x 3.88"
Power (bhp @ rpm)	450 @ 5200
Torque (lb-ft @ rpm*	490 @ 3700
Compression Ratio	9.6:1
Transmission	6-spd manual
Final Drive	3.07:1
Wheelbase	96.2"
Track (front/rear)	59.6"/60.6"
Overall Length	176.7"
Overall Width	75.7"
Overall Height	47.0"
Curb Weight	3460 lbs
Weight distribution	46/54
Ground Clearance	5.0"
Coefficient of Drag (cd)	0.35
Fuel Tank Capacity	19 gallons
Engine Oil	8 quarts
Frame	Tubular space frame
Front Suspension	Independent, unequal length A-arms
Front Shocks	Coil-over, low pressure gas Adjustable rebound
Front Anti-roll Bar	Tubular 27 mm diameter
Rear Suspension	Independent, unequal length A-arms
Rear shocks	Coil-over, low pressure gas Adjustable rebound
Rear Anti-roll bar	Tubular 22 mm diameter
Steering	Power rack & pinion
Front Brakes	13" vented discs with 4-piston calipers
Rear Brakes	13" vented discs with single piston calipers
Front Wheels	10" x 18" forged aluminum
Rear Wheels	13" x 18" forged aluminum
Front Tires	Michelin Pilot Sport 275/35 ZR18
Rear Tires	Michelin Pilot Sport 335/30 ZR18
Tire pressure	29 psi
Notes	2001-02 w/ABS

I Bought a 1999 Viper

Dan Moody waited until 1999 to buy his Viper because of all the improvements made that year.

It was the end of 1999 when I decided to buy a Viper GTS. The color I wanted was silver with blue stripes. Ninety-nine was the last year for this color combination. There were only forty-something non-ACR models built in this color combination, and I found the last new one available.

A number of significant improvements were added in 1999: electrically adjustable side mirrors, an inside hatch release, but the most important to me was the new 18-inch smooth five-spoke wheels.

I love the Viper's bad-ass looks and its bad-ass power! It's like driving a street-legal race car. It has the power of a big block Chevelle I once owned and the handling of my Triumiles per hour Spitfire. But it's way more fun!

You have to be really careful not to scrape the spoiler going in and out of driveways. And the Viper can bite. First gear will spin you around before you know it. I recommend going to Viper Days driving school. It's the best thing you can do to protect yourself, your passenger, and your Viper!

If you join the VCA, you'll receive a warm welcome and have a chance to learn about your new Viper. We've made a lot of friends and memories through the club. One of my favorite moments was when we shared our Vipers with some kids who were in the hospital. Climbing in and out of the Vipers made them forget about their illnesses for awhile.

I Bought a 1999 ACR

Fred Kinder has owned five Vipers, three of which he still owns, so he's had experience with the RT/10, GTS, ACR, and the new SRT-10. How does the ACR compare?

I wanted the best possible performance for street, open track, and autocrossing, so I bought the ACR when it came out. The ride is a lot firmer. Compared to the new SRT-10, it rides like a truck. It's nice that the shocks are adjustable for performance tuning, but you really need a race car suspension expert to help you set it up. Some of the earlier cars had shocks that rattled over bumpy roads.

I've had Caldwell Development, Inc., modify the engine for more performance, Dan Cragin install a fire-suppression system and custom exhaust system, and Eric Messley set up the suspension. Some of my most memorable times in a Viper are driving the ACR on the open track. What a thrill!

Personally, I think the added cost of the ACR package would be better spent on driving schools and aftermarket modifications.

What They Said in 1999

Who says racing doesn't improve the breed anymore? In the case of the Dodge Viper ACR (American Club Racer), the Viper GTS has been reworked to make it the basis for an SCCA Class T1 club racer, and it incorporates some of the lessons Viper engineers learned while chasing the FIA GT2 racing title during the past two years. These cars are usable on the road yet rather marvelous on the track.

By removing the radio and speakers, the air conditioning, and the fog lamps, Viper engineers have made the ACR sixty pounds lighter than the normal GTS coupe. Like the GTS, the ACR has 275/35 front and 335/30 rear Michelin Pilot Sport tires, but the eighteen-inch wheels are supplied by BBS. The (standard) coil-over-damper units are replaced by the Meritor springs and the adjustable, alloy-bodied, and gas-charged Koni dampers fitted to the GTS/R race cars. Last but not least, the 8.0-liter pushrod V-10 engine has slightly more power and torque, courtesy of smooth instead of ribbed intake tubes, a revised airbox, and K&N air filters.

In many ways, the ACR is similar in concept to the recent GT2 special edition. The difference, however, is that the ACR is intended to be raced. As soon as you drive the ACR on the track, you can see that the extra expenditure is worth it and that you're paying for a lot of expertise and development. The ACR is the nicest GTS I've driven, a wonderfully fluent track car that utterly belies its size and is both faster and easier to drive than the standard GTS. The ACR feels really well sorted, as if the people who did the chassis tuning know racing and know cars.

Whereas a standard GTS virtually pitches itself into tail-out mode at the touch of the gas pedal, you have to be brutal with the ACR to get it sideways. If the ACR had been the work of many a tuning shop, the improved track handling would have been offset by a bone-crunching ride, but we found the ride to be firm yet hardly shocking on badly worn freeways.

What we really love about these cars is that they end up being more than just tuning packages: They feel like racing cars on the track and yet are perfectly usable on the street.

~*Automobile Magazine*, November 1998

Standard '99 GTS *Chrysler*

When we bring a Dodge Viper GTS to the test track, a long line of thrill riders magically materializes. Suddenly, I'm Chief Imagineer for Mr. Mac's Wild Ride, ready to tantalize every track employee from general manager to janitor. Step aboard.

My victims, uh, passengers often stammer nervously as they hunt for the unique out-board mounted seat buckle. The instant it clicks, I rev the 8.0-liter V-10 to three grand and dump the clutch. All talk ends. The Dodge catapults forward in an opposite-lock, tire-smoking power slide, its uneven-firing pushrod mill bellowing like a WWII Merlin.

I snatch a redline shift to second and ask, "When should I get on the brakes?" Most shout "Now!" I punctuate my response ("Oh, no, not now.") by slamming it into third and going back to wide-open throttle. The riders stammer, "Nownownow!" as I grab fourth and pass 120 miles per hour.

"Oh, the brakes," you say? Threshold braking pitches the rider forward against the shoulder belt. Just as we come to a halt, before my rider catches his breath, I do a serious, no-wheelspin launch. The Viper's 450 horses hurl us 0–60 miles per hour in 4.1 seconds, launch us toward the slalom course. Exiting the cones at over 80 miles per hour, I wag the tail just for grins. A hard right turn and we're running around the skidpad, the asphalt version of a centrifuge, though the 1999 Viper's new 18-inch tires produce 0.03 g less grip than the old 17s. Then I attempt a lap of power oversteer around the pad: Controlling a fully loose GTS in this manner is like balancing a grape on a knife.

On the run to top speed, wind and engine noise assault the ears. The side windows seem ready to blow out. The snake bucks and bounds, almost bottoming out at 186.8 miles per hour. That's 5.8 miles per hour slower than a 1998, a surprising decrease.

Finally, I slow to the banking's neutral speed and rest my hands on my thighs. At 135 miles per hour. Next in line!

~*Motor Trend*, July 1999

Changes to all 1999 GTSs

No more fog light covers.

New satin-finish aluminum interior trim.

Dodge added a remote hatch release.

New 18-inch five-spoke wheels featured a smooth, wide spoke design.

Power mirrors added.

Colors were red, silver, and black. Optional silver stripes on the black and red cars, blue on the silver cars.

ACR option deleted fog lamps, A/C, and audio system, though wiring for audio system was still in place.

Under the hood, the ACR used a smooth tube intake with K&N air filters.

Power mirrors added.

18-inch BBS wheels with Michelin Pilot Sport tires came on the ACR.

Adjustable suspension.

Inside, the ACR featured
five-point harnesses and
a dash plaque.

Ron Kimball

2000 GTS

Collectibility: **

In 2000, the engine was revised to meet stricter emissions regulations. Though power output remained the same, the engine used a smoother, milder cam with 6 degrees less overlap, and revised "high leakdown" lifters. Forged aluminum pistons were replaced with eutectic cast-aluminum pistons, which were stronger and lighter.

The only other changes were the colors. Red and black continued and Steel Gray (code PS6) made a one-year appearance replacing silver. Any of the colors could be ordered with optional dual silver stripes. The ACR option continued.

What They Said in 2000

Truth told, there's not much new on the 2000 Viper GTS. Sure, you can order your snake in a new steel gray hue or get the new child seat tether mounts (Who thinks this is a family car?), but other than that, it's the same old Viper GTS. But believe us: that's good.

What's it like to actually drive an ACR? Smack down the right pedal and you're in for a 4.16-sec 0–60 thrill ride. The Viper's V-10 is so powerful it's downright violent. Mash the center pedal, and you'll get instantly wide-eyed as the massive front tires like to lock up and slide, thanks to no ABS (slated for 2001 models, however). The far-left pedal is easy to modulate—not too much clutch pressure in traffic, yet grabby enough to deliver effective feathering on traction limited surfaces.

Though the ACR delivers a Tyson-like punch at the track, on the road it remains relatively civil. In sixth gear with the V-10 chugging at a mere 1800 rpm, the Viper slithers along at just over 80 miles per hour. Sure, a Viper GTS (ACR or not) is far from the best daily driver choice, but then again it was never intended for such. Rather, it's meant to put some serious drive into your day—and that it does with a bite.

~Motor Trend, November 2000

I Bought a 2000 Viper

In a way, Zuzana Kukol epitomizes the kind of woman you'd expect to own a Viper. In addition to her snake, she drives a lifted Yukon and an H2 Hummer. She has three Bengal Tigers as pets. And she's licensed to own and carry a fully automatic machine gun. She's just a little out there.

I love everything about the Viper: the looks, the sex appeal, the power, the torque, and the feel! It's a true all-American muscle car! I've driven/owned other fast cars, like the Corvette, BMW 850i, Mercedes 500 SL, and Jaguar XJR—but the Viper is in a different class. It's like no other car. Right out of the box, it's a race car you can drive on the street.

I chose a 2000 model because I wanted the newest Viper I could get *without* ABS. I didn't want all that safety stuff. Luckily, the local Dodge dealer had a used hot red coupe in stock.

Its main attraction is also its main quirk—all that power means it can get loose in the back—this forces you to be an aggressive yet careful driver—I love that. It's impossible to drive slowly, even if you try. I tried to drive slowly at a local Porsche club rally where Ferrari, BMW, Corvette, Viper, and Mercedes clubs were invited. I was still the fastest. So they awarded me handcuffs to put on myself, since police failed to do it that day. If you respect the power this car has, it is *fun* to drive.

Taking it on the track for Viper Days is a lot of fun. Beyond that, it's just fun to watch people's reactions when they see 100 Vipers driving down the freeway together during a club event.

Being a woman Viper owner, I do get respect from men who love cars. I find it funny when I have a male passenger with me, people assume it's not my car. At a race in Las Vegas, a NASCAR groupie walked up to my male passenger, a local Viper technician, and asked him while pointing to me, "Why do you let *her* drive this car???" I just had to laugh.

John Penn's experience shows the importance of going to a Dodge dealer who specializes in Vipers.

I'd always wanted to purchase a Viper, though in the beginning, I thought it wouldn't make much sense—after all, when it was introduced, it was topless and windowless. At the time I lived in a state with weather. So when the Viper GTS was introduced, I was completely hooked and ready to buy.

I was set on purchasing a new Viper. I shopped for Vipers for many years, but was rarely taken seriously by the dealers. When I was taken seriously, the dealer prices were often thousands, even tens of thousands of dollars over sticker. They were never able to provide any information to me about the car or purchasing or insurance. Then one day while I was visiting a Dodge dealer, a young man named Brian Angen introduced me to Terri, his Mom, who owned two Vipers. My Viper dream finally became a reality.

Terri told me about the Viper Club of America, the meetings, and the website. I had never even heard of the Viper Club before. That day, I went to the website and found comments by owners and a list of recommended dealers. The first dealer I called was in Los Angeles. He was incredibly helpful, knew about the car, and offered me the most reasonable price I had heard in my entire search. I ordered a Steel Gray GTS with silver stripes by phone that day.

Having gone through the process of ordering from the factory, some things I found important are:

1. You'll want to know when a particular model year is being produced, since it doesn't coincide with the calendar year.

2. You never know exactly when it will be delivered.

3. There is a whole series of codes that the factory uses to keep the dealer abreast of the build status of your vehicle.

4. It's possible to pick your Viper up at the plant and drive it home!

Since I ordered my Viper, my window sticker came printed with my name on it—"Built Exclusively For John Penn."

Although I've heard many people tell me the Viper is not a daily driver, living in California, I drive mine every day I can, except when it rains.

New Steel Gray color available with or without silver stripes.

Revised engine with milder camshaft and revised lifters to meet stricter emissions regulations.

Maurice Q. Liang

2001 GTS

Collectibility: ★★★★

The big news for 2001 was the addition of a three-channel ABS. Vipers had been long criticized for locking up their right front brakes under hard braking, so Team Viper decided it was time to add ABS.

For colors, red continued to be available with or without silver stripes. Black and steel gray were dropped, replaced by a deep metallic sapphire blue (code PBW—a one-year color) and a bright Viper Race Yellow (code PYR). Sapphire GTSs were available with optional silver stripes, while yellow coupes were available with optional black stripes. All colors continued to be available with standard black interior or the Cognac leather interior.

The ACR option continued to be available on all GTSs.

If you plan to take your Viper to the track, the 2001 and 2002 models are the best because of ABS.

I Bought a 2001 Viper

Linda Andres is another one of those rare female owners. She loves her Viper.

This car is fast. It is fast. It is fun. It is beautiful. Did I mention it is fast? We had a 1997 GTS and sold it—but I really missed driving it, so we bought a 2001 ACR. It's a little stiffer than the standard GTS—the standard GTS was a little easier to drive around town. The ACR is fantastic on an open stretch of road, though.

Standard 2001 GTS has 5-spoke wheels and fog lamps. *Chrysler*

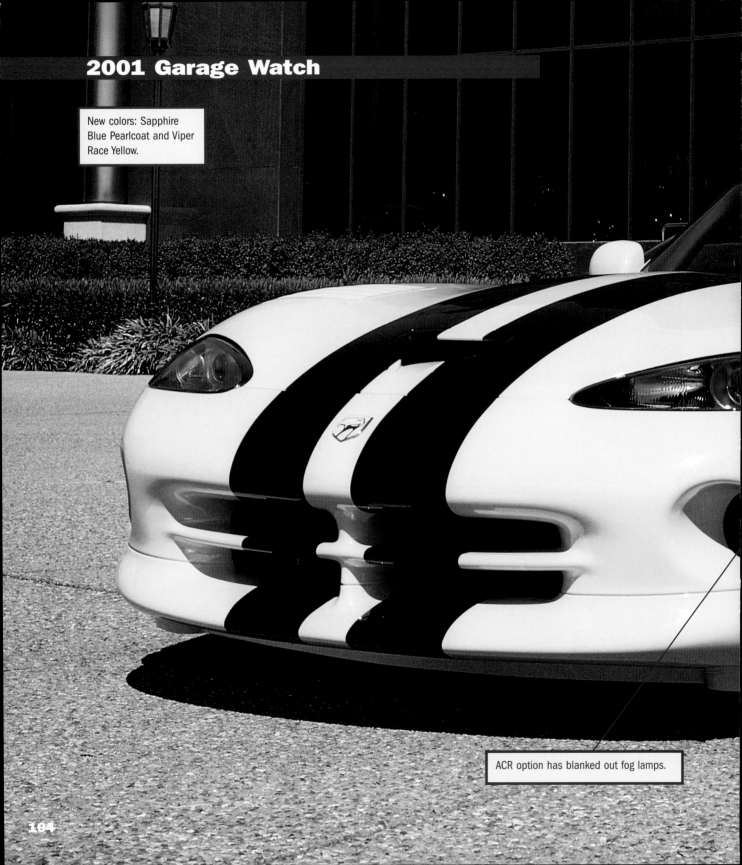

New colors: Sapphire Blue Pearlcoat and Viper Race Yellow.

ACR option has blanked out fog lamps.

MUSEUM

ACR option has BBS wheels.

ABS brake lines are black, while non-ABS brake lines are silver.

Ron Kimball

2002 GTS

Collectibility: ★★★★

Two thousand-two marked the final year for the original-style Vipers. The only changes were colors. Sapphire blue was replaced by Graphite Metallic (code PDR), available with optional silver stripes. Red, with optional silver stripes, and yellow, with optional black stripes, continued to be available.

To mark the end of the generation, Dodge built 360 Final Edition models, in the red with white stripe paint scheme of the American Le Mans–winning GTS/Rs. This special edition was less elaborate than the GT2 from 1998, lacking all the aerodynamic pieces. Inside, the interior featured a dash plaque and red stitching on the steering wheel and shift knob. An owner's registry dedicated to these Final Edition cars can be found at www.FEViper.com.

What They Said in 2002

The next-generation Dodge Viper goes on sale in August. It'll be a convertible powered by a 500-horsepower, 8.3-liter V-10 engine.

To me, the appeal of the Viper always has been its brute force. Hopefully, that won't change.

Ten years ago, when the first Viper RT/10 roadster rolled off the assembly line, it was pure exhilaration. Primal, I called it. Here was a car with no air bags and no anti-lock brakes. It had a hard-to-harness canvas top and a noisy ride that made conversation and high-fidelity sounds impossible to enjoy. It had no air conditioning and a tiny trunk.

What it did have was a 400-horsepower V-10 engine with a great, raspy rumble and a body that looked like a permanently flexed muscle.

That was enough for me.

In 1996, Dodge introduced the Viper GTS coupe, showing it off first in Monterey at a Viper owners' meet. I recently drove a yellow and black, 2001 version of that car—the 2002 model was little changed.

Horsepower has grown to 450, which is a good thing. I can't deny that the Viper remains a vehicle that's very much dedicated to driving fast. That was especially true in our test model, which came with the $10,000 ACR competition group package that deleted many of the niceties (radio, AC, fog lamps) and had a competition suspension.

Dodge has sold some 14,000 Vipers since 1992, and I'm sure almost every owner got one because of the car's potent engine. Let's just hope the new version coming late this year isn't *too* civilized.

~*San Jose Mercury News*, June 14, 2002

I Bought a 2002 Viper

Al Lai jumped from one end of the spectrum to the other, when he traded his early roadster for a Final Edition GTS coupe. Al tells us how they compare.

I have been the original owner of two Dodge Vipers. The first Viper I purchased was an early 1993 RT/10 roadster. I was attracted to the Viper because of its muscular design and its outrageous performance. I also felt and still feel that the design of the car is timeless. I have owned several different sports cars—but none can compare to the Viper. It has a distinctive look that appeals to people young and old.

Initially, the Viper was only offered as a roadster and only came in red with a gray leather interior. No ABS, no roll-up windows, no air conditioning, and only a simple fold-up top.

While I really enjoyed driving the car when the weather was nice, I never drove it in the rain. I felt that this was a "fair weather car" due to the difficulty in putting on the fold-up roof—if one did not put the roof on correctly, the roof could fly off while driving.

Many years later, I heard that Dodge was producing the Final Edition GTS to commemorate the end of the second-generation Vipers and their consecutive wins at the Daytona American Le Mans Series. Although design and performance were still the main items that drew my attention to the Final Edition, the comfort and convenience the GTS offered sold me on it. Also, the fact that this car came in red with white stripes as standard (stripes were an option in other years) was another thing that sold me on this car.

Driving the Final Edition is very comfortable. The seat adjustments along with the adjustable pedals (not available on the early Vipers) make it more enjoyable and easy to drive. Also, this car has a reverse-gear lock-out, something my early RT/10 didn't have. (Nothing like going from fourth to fifth gear and hitting reverse instead!) The only drawback to the Final Edition is that it does not come with sidepipes, which I liked on my RT/10.

I enjoy driving my Final Edition, though I often find myself missing the "wind in my hair and the sun in my face" experience of the RT/10. What I do *not* miss, however, are the cramped knees, the hot sun, and the cold wind. All in all, I like the Final Edition better. I can drive "rain or shine," and all I have to do when I miss the wind is lower my electric windows!

2002 Garage Watch

Dodge built 360 Final Edition models in red with white stripes to commemorate the end of GTS production and the GTS/R wins at Daytona.

Final Edition dash plaque.

Final Edition interiors featured red stitching on shift knob and steering wheel. Note power mirror adjustment on left of console, toggle-style power window switches, and air bag cutoff switch on right.

Maurice Q. Liang

An all-new Viper was produced in 2003.

Chapter 5

2003–2004
SRT/10

The third generation of Vipers began in 2003 with the all-new SRT-10, which stood for Street Racing Technology, 10-cylinder. The SRT-10 featured a new body-style, now with a manual folding convertible top, which didn't take up trunk space. The wheelbase increased 2.6 inches, but the overall length was actually 1 inch shorter than the original RT/10. Dodge listened to customers and gave them what they asked for: more horsepower, better brakes, improved interior materials, and a more useble car.

The V-10 was enlarged to 8.3 liters, which produced 500 horsepower and 525 ft-lb of torque. In addition, the engine had to meet more stringent emissions controls, and weight was reduced. Dodge engineers found a way to put back side exhausts, which had been absent since 1996. The exhaust found was improved by placing a cross-over pipe between the two sides.

Brakes were always the weak spot of the Viper, and Dodge was determined to fix them. Rotors were increased an inch in diameter and coupled with a three-channel ABS system, the Viper could now stop after 60 mph at only 97 feet.

Inside, the interior was completely redesigned, with the tach front and center, surrounded by a smaller speedometer and gas gauge, while auxiliary gauges cascaded down the center stack similar to a race car. Adding to the race car theme, Dodge used a start button for the engine. The pedal cluster was electrically adjustable, and finally a dead pedal was available for the driver to rest their left foot. And, unlike Vipers in the past, you could now adjust the temperature in the car. The sound of the stereo was also vastly improved over the first- and second-generation cars.

While handling was always impressive, Dodge engineers redesigned the suspension to give more progressive handling at the limit, so breaking loose was less sudden and more manageable. While front wheels remained at 18 inches in diameter, the rear wheels increased to 19 inches. New Michelin tires also contributed to the improved handling, while eliminating the need for a spare tire. Sizes were 275/35 ZR18's in the front and 345/30 ZR19's in the rear.

A squared-off, edgier style replaced the smooth, voluptuous body of the older car. While the Dodge cross-hair in the grill was made bolder, some of the car's trademarks had been eliminated, such as the: curvy side vents, the "speaker-grills" in the hood, the curvaceous waist, and the sport bar. The new car looked meaner, at least from the front. This was even reflected in the snake emblem. The old, mischievous-looking "Sneaky Pete" snake logo was replaced with a tougher looking snake dubbed "Fang," now available only in charcoal, instead of being color-keyed to the body.

Some felt the updated style resembled too many other cars, while the rest felt the look was more refined and less cartoonish than the old car. Regardless, the SRT-10 succeeded in attracting new buyers who preferred the overall sophistication of the car.

But if you think the Viper has gone soft, remember that it still has no cruise control, no traction control, no automatic transmission, and no cup holders. Compared to the older series, the SRT-10 is slightly faster, handles better, is more comfortable, and is more usable as a daily driver. The only question is whether or not you like the new style.

2003 SRT-10

Collectibility: **

For the first year of production, the color choices were solid red (LRN), black (MX3), and metallic silver (VA9). Red made up about 50 percent of production and the rest was split between silver and black. All cars came with black interiors and black tops.

The quickest way to visually identify a 2003 SRT-10 is by the black brake calipers. Like the older Vipers, the trunk was left in unfinished fiberglass but an optional carpet kit was available through Mopar parts to line the trunk.

Things to watch for are heat in the footwells, which remains an issue, although Dodge engineers are working on a solution. Headlights are known to flicker off and on, and a recall was issued to reprogram the computer.

A batch of SRT-10s built in spring of 2003 received valves, which were not ground correctly, causing a loss in horsepower. Dodge issued a recall to replace the valves. Be sure to check if the car you're considering was affected and if so, make sure the recall was followed.

Viper Specifications 2003–2004 SRT/10	
Engine	8.3 L V-10
Bore/Stroke	4.03" x 3.96"
Power (bhp @ rpm)	500 @ 5600
Torque (lb-ft @ rpm*	525 @ 4200
Compression Ratio	9.6:1
Transmission	6-spd manual
Final Drive	3.07:1
Wheelbase	98.8"
Track (front/rear)	57.8"/60.9"
Overall Length	175.6"
Overall Width	75.2"
Overall Height	47.6"
Curb Weight	3380 lbs
Weight distribution	48/52
Ground Clearance	5.1"
Coefficient of Drag (cd)	0.43
Fuel Tank Capacity	18.5 gallons
Engine Oil	10.5 quarts
Frame	Tubular space frame
Front Suspension	Independent, unequal length A-arms
Front Shocks	Coil-over, high pressure gas Adjustable rebound
Front Anti-roll Bar	Tubular 26mm diameter
Rear Suspension	Independent, unequal length A-arms
Rear shocks	Coil-over, high pressure gas Adjustable rebound
Rear Anti-roll bar	Tubular 22mm diameter
Steering	Power rack & pinion
Front Brakes	14" vented discs with 4-piston calipers & ABS
Rear Brakes	14" vented discs with 4-piston calipers & ABS
Front Wheels	10" x 18" forged aluminum
Rear Wheels	13" x 19" forged aluminum
Front Tires	Michelin ZP 275/35 ZR18
Rear Tires	Michelin ZP 345/30 ZR19
Tire pressure	29 psi

I Bought a 2003 SRT-10

The new Viper SRT-10 has been winning over new buyers. Tom Callero switched from a Corvette to the new Viper SRT-10.

On March 10, 2003, I took possession of a new Dodge Viper SRT-10, and the incredible experience began. I have owned many high-performance cars in the past from Corvettes to Porsches and although they are wonderful automobiles I did not realize the true meaning of performance personified until I drove my new SRT-10.

The first time you fire up the SRT-10 you understand why people are drawn to the car. It has a feeling of unleashed fury that you control, and yes, it can be controlled because the car is so well balanced. The engine numbers are nothing short of amazing. It has 505 cubic inches, 500 horsepower, 525 lb-ft of torque. It's the first time in automotive history a car has reached this triple-threat milestone. The throttle response is race car-like because the car has amazing torque at just about any rpm. The car races to 0–60 in under 4 seconds, and it does the quarter mile in the 12-second range. Enough with the numbers. How does it feel to drive this true American muscle car?

When you enter the race-inspired cockpit you feel safe and secure because it has a shape and form that fits the human body well. The controls, gauges, and dashboard are all right there in well-thought-out positions. To start the car, you push a red button just like in the old days, and the engine roars to life. The engine tone is deep and throaty. The car shakes a little, letting you know you have a beast that is about to be unleashed.

In comparison to another American muscle car, the Corvette, the Dodge Viper SRT-10 takes no prisoners. The Viper simply outperforms the Corvette in all aspects of performance. The Viper feels more stable at high speeds, and the braking is more precise. The handling is much more stable with less roll. The Viper accelerates faster and continues to pull throughout the rpm range.

If you want a car that is fun to drive, gives you a sense of freedom, and will be the talk of the town, then this is the car for you!

What They Said in 2003

With the 2003 Viper SRT-10—the SRT stands for Street and Racing Technology, you know what the 10 stands for—Dodge has addressed the lion's share of the previous Viper's failings. By punching out the pushrod V10 from 7,990 to 8,277 cc, PVO was able to achieve a 50 horsepower increase to 500 horsepower at 5,600 rpm. This increased capacity also led to a sizeable 35 lb-ft increase in torque to a Goliath 525 lb-ft, 90% of which can be accessed from as low as 1,500 rpm.

Thanks to that wheelbase increase, there is noticeably more space inside. Extra room was also given to the footwells; a dead pedal now resides next to the clutch pedal. The high bolstered leather seats are truly first-rate. Ergonomically speaking, the interior is much better laid out, with everything of importance coming much easier to hand and eye. The tachometer is centrally located. Overall, the feel and quality of the materials used has taken a few big steps in the right direction. The interior is still not on par with its German rivals, but it's much closer.

Make no bones about it; the new Viper is a shockingly fast car. The bigger engine definitely pulls harder from lower rpm than the previous V10, delivering acceleration that will take your breath away in any gear except the overly tall sixth. The PVO folks say the SRT-10 will accelerate to 60 in under 4 seconds.

Even more impressive, however, is the way the new Viper handles and brakes. Its turn-in has that all-of-a-piece feel of a well-sorted sports car. What's more, there is more information being passed along to the driver through the steering wheel and seat bottom.

Another item on the wish list of Viper owners was the return of the side-pipe exhaust system. Dodge duly obliged. Thanks to an intricate dual cross-over pipe setup, the SRT-10 doesn't sound like a UPS truck, as did the first RT/10; the new Viper sounds great. But the engineers did not solve the other problem that plagued those early side-pipe Vipers—excessive heat.

Dodge actually had a whole year to fix the problem because the entire run of 2003 Vipers has been presold to existing Viper owners, many of whom will view their toasty side sills as a source of pride, a sure sign of bad-to-the-bone muscle car toughness.

~Sports Car International, January 2003

If you're lucky enough to own a Dodge Viper, you already know it does something to you. It seems to make you want more—as in more than one. Every owner that responded to our AutoFile survey has plunked down cash for multiple copies of the now 11-year-old car, and most garages have more than one. As one owner put it, "Once you've been bitten, no other snake will do."

No other car under $100K can get within spitting distance of the Viper's numbers. Our tight, 490-foot, eight cone slalom tends to punish cars of size. The Viper SRT-10 blows all of that thinking away. At 49.0 miles per hour, the Viper has not only taken over the title of the quickest through the slalom, but nothing we've tested even comes close. The now-relegated-to-second-best Porsche 911 Turbo only reached 48.1 miles per hour.

Thanks in part to the addition of a long-awaited antilock braking system, the SRT-10 requires just 109 feet to stop from 60 miles per hour—and does so with virtually no dive. That puts the Viper into supercar territory.

Owners had nothing but glowing things to say about this latest Viper, raving endlessly about its power, handling, braking, etc. Most also liked that this Viper roadster now wears a real convertible top, and many pointed out improvements in things like the stereo, climate control system and interior comfort. Somewhat surprisingly, though every respondent was a self-proclaimed Viper nut, not all were as completely bowled over by its styling as its performance.

Given all that fanaticism, it came as little surprise that most owners said they considered no other vehicles. Said one: "I could pay less and get less, or I could pay more and get less. There are no other choices."

~AutoWeek, June 9, 2003

All new design for 2003.

Some 2003 SRT-10's received incorrectly ground valves, resulting in a loss in horse-power. A recall was issued. If the car you are considering is affected, check to be sure the recall was performed.

New 500-horsepower, 525 lb-ft torque V-10

New race car inspired racecar design.

New larger-diameter wheels (18 inches in front, 19 inches in rear).

Folding convertible top stores below deck lid without taking up trunk space.

Air diffusers in the rear are vulnerable to damage when backing up to a curb. (Add inset photo)

New larger, much improved brakes.

2004 SRT-10

Collectibility: **

Since the 2003 SRT-10 was all new, there were minimal changes to the 2004 model. Vipers received new trunk carpet, an improved version of the Mopar carpet kit that was previously an accessory, red brake calipers, and a convertible boot cover that folded up into a small bag when not in use.

In addition to red, black, and silver, 200 Vipers were built in white (code BWA). The white paint is the brightest white ever developed for use on an automobile. All white cars came with the optional "Mamba" (named after a deadly snake) interior, which was a two-tone black with red accents on the knee blockers, door panels, center console, shift knob, steering wheel, and emergency brake handle, with a special numbered plaque on the center console. Mamba's were not built in sequence, so the number on the plaque does not indicate build sequence or coordinate with the VIN. The snake emblem on the steering wheel and the hood crest also featured a red shield instead of the standard charcoal shield. The emblems on the front fenders featured a silver "Viper" and red "SRT-10" logo, while the emblems on the rear bumpers remained body color white. One other minor difference with the white cars was that the fender lip that ran under the edge of the hood was blacked out to better hide the black bolt heads.

With special-trim cars like this, replacement parts become a challenge in the future. If you plan to keep your car for a long time, it's wise to buy spares of all the unique parts that are likely to wear out, like the steering wheel and shift knob.

I Bought a 2004 SRT-10

Steve Ferguson is co-founder and a past national and regional president of the Viper Club of America and has owned a 1993 RT/10 until now. He has number 200 of the 200 white Viper SRT-10s on order.

I ordered my first Viper because no one else made a brutal sports car that was simply all about power and not about ANYTHING else. In my humble (not) opinion, a sports car with a cup holder means you need caffeine either from coffee or cola. But with a Viper the caffeine is IN THE CAR!

The one and only reason my first Viper will be with me until death-do-we-part is because it is a REAL sports car—no ABS, no real top, no windows, and no AIR! No other manufacturer has ever nor will they ever have the gall to build such a non-sensible car, and that is what I love most about my 1993.

You may have noticed I have a 2004 on order. That represents a decade of begging and pleading for a white Viper with every executive I have been in contact with at Chrysler since my first introduction to the top brass almost 10 years ago. Up until last year, every Chrysler executive would actually make fun of me for requesting white. "It would make the Viper look like an appliance," they'd say.

Well late in 2002 I was blessed with the ultimate gift from the ultimate enthusiast—manufacturer relationship. A high-ranking executive at Chrysler actually brought me in the design studio to show me a future Viper color. The color was the white I had lobbied for my entire Viper life! I will never be able to express my gratitude nor will I ever be able to truly explain how much seeing my dream unveiled before my eyes means to me.

My advice to those who want to buy a Viper is simple—go to a local VCA event, meet the members, look at the Vipers and see all the differences between the model years, and get ready to change your LIFE. Once you have your Viper, whatever you do, at least experience it once in its truest and most sensual sense by taking it to a high-performance driving event.

What They Said in 2004

Enough talk. You demanded a legit, track-test showdown between America's 500-horse contenders (the Viper SRT-10 and the Ford GT). We're here to serve.

Sorry, bow-tie boosters. Chevy's Corvette sat this one out. Among the world's best-performance values, even the 405-horsepower Z06 lacks the beans to tee up on this turf.

Neither the Ford nor the Dodge requires a shift before hitting 60 miles per hour, a key ingredient to their respective 3.6- and 3.9-second performances. Indeed, 60 arrives just at the crankshaft-straining first-gear redline in both machines. The Ford's 0.3 second advantage may not sound like a big margin, but in acceleration parlance, it's a lifetime.

Things tightened up farther down the drag strip. The GT remained a bumper ahead all the way to 100, which the Viper reached in 8.4 seconds and the GT hit in just 8.1 seconds. By the time both cars hit the quarter-mile traps, the Viper caught its breath and managed to nip the GT by just one-hundredth of a second with a slightly lower trap speed of 123.63 versus the GT's 124.31. *Yeow.* Without electronic timing, it'd be way to close to call.

Standing on the GT's pedal from 60 miles per hour nailed six stops all at less than 115 feet. Stopping the Viper was even more like hitting a wall, taking a staggering short 97 feet to haul down from 60 to 0. And, like the GT, it could repeat the deed over and over, with no heat-related fade.

Few hot rides can do the 600-foot cone dance as quickly as these two-seaters; anything over 70 miles per hour is serious stuff. This pair qualified, with the Ford nipping the Dodge by 1.1 miles per hour (71.5 versus 70.4). The GT is so together it somehow feels like it's going slower than it actually is.

The previous-generation Viper had a reputation for punishing slow-reacting and inattentive drivers. It had high limits, but they never reached or communicated to the cockpit in anything resembling a progressive manner. The SRT-10 has much-improved on-limit handling behavior and feedback. But the chassis still feels a tad numb, at least as compared with the mongoose-quick GT.

This pair of 500-horsepower players are screaming-bargains when compared with high-ticket foreign goods. It's worth noting that the Viper delivers objective performance generally on par with that of the GT for about 40 percent less money. The heritage-inspired Ford packs more tech and is a more sophisticated piece, so its higher price is justified—but that in no way diminishes the SRT-10's impressive punch-per-penny quotient.

~*Motor Trend*, January 2004

Changes to all 1999 GTSs

New red brake calipers.

New trunk carpet.

Convertible cover.

200 Mamba special editions were produced in 2004, all white with black and red interiors. Red, black, and silver continued as standard colors.

Red hood emblem replaces charcoal emblem on Mamba edition.

Limited edition of 200 white cars, all with the two-tone "Mamba" interior, which included red accents on the knee blockers, door panels, steering wheel, center console, shift knob, and e-brake handle, as well as red stitching for the seats and steering wheel and the Viper logo on the headrest.

Silver "Viper" and red "SRT/10" replace body color emblems on the Mamba edition.

Maurice Q. Liang

Since paint was optional on Competition Coupes many customers created their own wild color schemes. *Maurice Q. Liang*

Chapter 6

Race Vipers

Dodge realized that for a performance car to have true heritage, it needed to win races. As a result, the Viper GTS/R was introduced and designed to compete at endurance races like 24 hours of Le Mans and Daytona. The intent was to use as much of the stock Viper as possible to improve the breed, rather than build a completely new purpose-built race car.

The results were impressive, as Chrysler Viper Team ORECA chalked up numerous wins, including the FIA (Fédération Internationale de l'Automobile) GT2 Manufacturer's Championship in 1997 and 1998. As Lou Patane, then executive director, Chrysler Motorsports Operations said, "It truly has become one of the world's great racing marques. We are proud of the fact that the Viper GTS-R—a true production vehicle—was born and developed in-house at Chrysler and has proven itself as a world-class winner...twice." ORECA's drivers, Olivier Beretta and Pedro Lamy also captured the FIA GT2 Driver's title.

GTS/Rs were only sold to racing teams but some have ended up in collectors' hands. They should not be confused with the street-replica version known as the GT2 (see 1998 GTS) or the ACR (American Club Racer) option (see 1999 GTS).

For the third generation Viper, Dodge has built a track-only coupe version called the Competition Coupe. The Competition Coupe uses a modified chassis and the same basic V-10 engine from the road-going SRT-10. Unlike the GTS/R, which was built for international endurance racing, the Competition Coupe is aimed at club racing like the Viper Racing League and SCCA World Challenge series. Credentialed race teams can purchase Competition Coupes directly from the factory and receive factory support.

In collector car history, racing cars are often sought after as the ultimate collectible because of their limited production, ultimate performance, and their significance in the marque's history. Vipers are no exception.

GTS/R

Collectibility: *****

In 1995, Chrysler unveiled the Viper GTS/R (R is for racing) during the Pebble Beach Concours weekend in Monterey, California. Though intentionally based upon the street-going GTS, the GTS/R was a factory-built racing Viper that private teams could purchase, race, and win with. Factory parts and service support were offered to all Viper GTS/R race teams. The intent was to develop a racing history and tradition for Viper. And that they did.

Engineers continuously made improvements to the engines, aerodynamics, drivetrains, and suspensions on their factory cars, passing along the changes to customers. Consequently, almost every GTS/R built was a unique vehicle, and once built, each car continued to evolve.

Weighing as little as 2,500 pounds, the GTS/R came with engines ranging from 580 horsepower to 700 horsepower, depending upon the level of the engine and the inlet restrictor size. As Bob Lutz said, "When you enter a gunfight with the world's best and fastest GT cars, you bring a big gun."

While a number of teams raced the GTS/R, Team ORECA eventually emerged as the winning, factory-backed team. Hughes de Chaunac was the owner, and the winning drivers included Dave Donahue, Justin Bell, Tommy Archer, Luca Drudi, Olivier Beretta, Karl Wendlinger, and Dominique Dupuy.

According to Jeff Reece, from SRTs Vehicle Development group, the first seven GTS/Rs were built in the Viper shop. This included two engineering development vehicles that saw limited racing, four factory ORECA cars (including the first FIA GT Championship car and the first Le Mans winner), and one turnkey customer car that was delivered to the Taisan team in Japan. After that, all GTS/Rs were assembled by ORECA in southern France. To date, 52 GTS/Rs have been built and production continues (based on the 1996 GTS).

Some GTS/Rs have ended up in private hands and some are still owned by Chrysler. A factory-built race car, especially one that has racing history, is the ultimate collectible Viper. Restoration can be tricky, however, as the cars have evolved during the production life and parts on any given car could be rare or even unique.

The actual LeMans winning GTS-R in as-raced condition is on display at the Walter P. Chrysler museum in Auburn, Hills, MI.

What They Said About the GTS/R

Unlike NASCAR Nextel Cup cars, which employ nothing from their road-going namesakes, the Viper (GTS/R) utilizes a large number of off-the-shelf parts. This is largely because of the rules for Le Mans and the new-for 1997 FIA GT Championship, which replaces the BPR series. The regulations fit well with the GTSs race-car-for-the-street nature and Chrysler's stated desire to race what it sells.

Typical for racers, Team Viper plays coy with horsepower figures, but we estimate the 1996 version made a bit more than 650 horses, despite breathing through the required pair of intake restrictors. Who knows what it would make with an open intake!

The result is beyond-outrageous performance. Try 0–60 miles per hour in 2.9 seconds and 0–100 miles per hour in just 5.4 seconds with a 10.3 second/143.9-miles per hour quarter mile.

Race cars vary in friendliness: The GTS/R proved to be a bon ami. Controls are familiar and felt much like the street Viper GTS I'd driven from the chateau to the track. Although stiffly sprung, the GTS/R was fairly emotive—I easily sensed the onset of understeer before it became a problem. At higher speeds, the big rear wing and aggressive front splitter smeared the car to the road. Overall, the GTS/R was, I'm thankful, tolerant of driving errors—except, that is, when I was too aggressive with the throttle leaving tight corners. Then it would wag its tail as if to say, "Naughty, naughty."

Team Viper offers ready-to-race examples for the relatively bargain-basement price of $285,000, which is just $30,000 over last year's price. Of course, you'll need another $2 million—$4 million would be better—to seriously contest both Le Mans and the GT Championship.

~*Motor Trend*, April 1997

In its (first) full season of road racing, the Dodge Viper achieved what no other American production-based performance car ever has: a world GT championship.

Viper GTS/R coupes campaigned by France's Team Oreca, Chrysler's factory-backed Viper race team, won the 1997 FIA GT-2 Manufacturers' championship. Oreca posted seven wins and nine poles in 10 starts. The win makes Chrysler the first U.S. automaker to notch an FIA title using a production-based car designed and developed in-house.

~*Automotive Industries*, December 1997

Full roll cage.

580–700-horsepower
V-10 racing engine.

Mobil 1

DODGE

DODGE

MICHELIN

MIC

Air splitter.

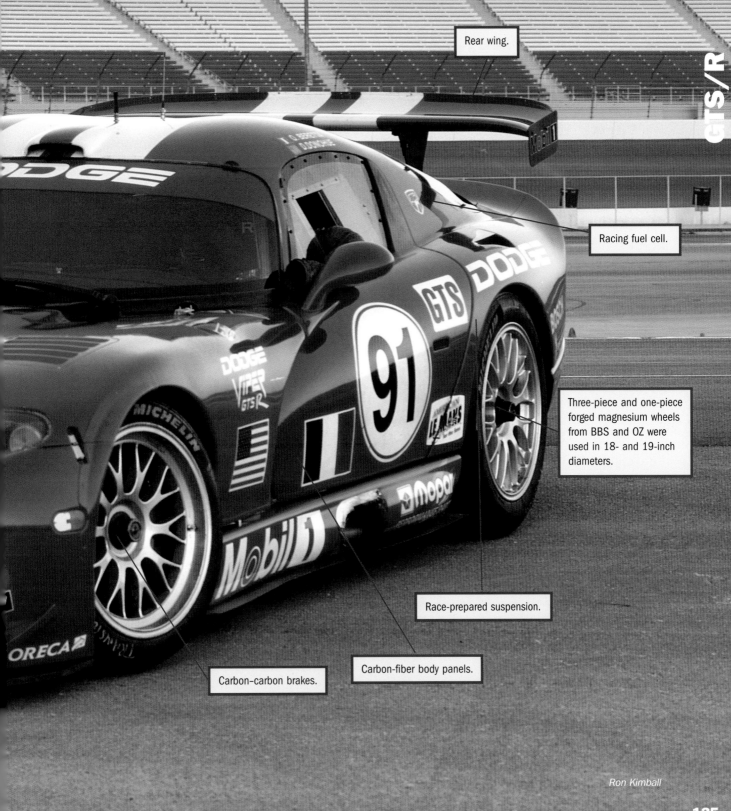

Rear wing.

Racing fuel cell.

Three-piece and one-piece forged magnesium wheels from BBS and OZ were used in 18- and 19-inch diameters.

Race-prepared suspension.

Carbon-fiber body panels.

Carbon–carbon brakes.

Ron Kimball

2003 Competition Coupe

Collectibility: *****

With only the convertible SRT-10 available, there was no track Viper for serious Viper racing enthusiasts. In response to the Viper Club of America members' requests for a track "kit car," SRT developed the track-only Competition Coupe, basing the body design on the 2000 GTS/R concept car.

Though based on the SRT-10's chassis, the Competition Coupe is a serious race car. The chassis is further reinforced, and a full roll cage installed. Fire-suppression system, air jacks, racing instrumentation, and racing suspension, are just a few of the modifications. The body is carbon-fiber. Fit and finish is a bit rough, but it's a race car.

The first batch of 32 Comp Coupes cost $100,000 each, a bargain when you considered the amount of equipment you got. Later cars went up in price. A total of 50 Competition Coupes were built in 2003. All were purchased directly from the factory, rather than through a Dodge dealer. To purchase a Comp Coupe, you had to qualify by showing proof of a racing license, past racing experience, and where you planned to race the Comp Coupe. SRT was not in the business of building garage queens. Nonetheless, a Comp Coupe will be one of the ultimate collectible Vipers sometime in the future.

Viper Specifications Competition Coupe	
Engine	8.3 L V-10
Bore/Stroke	4.03" x 3.96"
Power (bhp @ rpm)	520 @ 5600
Torque (lb-ft @ rpm*	540 @ 4600
Compression Ratio	9.6:1
Transmission	6-speed manual
Final Drive	3.07:1
Wheelbase	98.8"
Track (front/rear)	61.6"/64.6"
Overall Length	184.1"
Overall Width	77.2"
Overall Height	46.7"
Curb Weight	2950 lbs
Weight distribution	50/50
Ground Clearance	3"
Coefficient of Drag (cd)	0.4
Fuel Tank Capacity	26.4 gallons
Engine Oil	10 quarts
Frame	Tubular space frame w/FIA-legal cage
Front Suspension	Independent, unequal length A-arms
Front Shocks	Coil-over, monotube gas
	Adjustable compression & rebound
Front Anti-roll Bar	Driver-adjustable blade-type
Rear Suspension	Independent, unequal length A-arms
Rear shocks	Coil-over, monotube gas
	Adjustable compression & rebound
Rear Anti-roll bar	Tubular
Steering	Power rack & pinion
Front Brakes	14" vented discs with
	4-piston calipers & ABS
Rear Brakes	14" vented discs with
	4-piston calipers & ABS
Front Wheels	11" x 18" 3-piece BBS forged aluminum
Rear Wheels	14" x 19" 3-piece BBS forged aluminum
Front Tires	Michelin Pilot racing slicks 305/35 ZR18
Rear Tires	Michelin Pilot racing slicks 345/30 ZR19
Tire pressure	Varies

I Bought a Competition Coupe

In addition to being one of the premiere Viper dealers in the country, Bob Woodhouse is an avid racer. Naturally, he had to buy one of the Competition Coupes.

Being a previous Viper owner, I knew how much performance Vipers offer and having spent the last few years on race tracks with them, it was natural to decide to purchase a Competition Coupe. It's reliable, the chassis is rock-solid, the racing safety gear and Motec data-acquisition system are built in, and of course, it's faster! This is a great value. At $129,000, nothing comes close. Make no mistake, though. This is a serious race car, not a street car.

The car drives like it is on *rails. Steering and braking response are extremely quick. Compared to my GT-1 Viper Days race car, the shifter, clutch, and brake are all low pressure and easy to operate. It* has a very stiff suspension, which means it often takes a new driver some time to get acquainted before going all-out. For crash safety purposes, the seat is fixed, which makes it necessary to scramble for cushions when the car is being raced by multiple drivers.

Speaking from experience, the Comp Coupe is safe and strong. During a Speed World Challenge GT race at Road America, a Corvette got loose on the outside of Turn 8 and T-boned another Viper Competition Coupe. As part of the chain reaction, my Comp Coupe hit the rear of the stopped Corvette at 77 miles per hour! Yet, I survived with no problems.

If you are a track hound, this is for you. If you do more on the street, buy a Viper that is legal to carry a plate.

What They Said About the Competition Coupe

"The original GTS/R program was to build a production-based race car with the ability to compete at the highest level of international competition," Eric Petersen [CC Development Engineer] explains. "This Competition Coupe is a car for the Viper Club of America guys who race, to have something from the factory that is exactly spec with a sealed engine. It is for competition based on the driver's ability and not the preparation level of the cars."

Petersen said the Competition Coupe is intended for use in the Viper Racing League, SCCA World Challenge and Grand-Am Cup events. Initially priced at $100,000, the first 32 Competition Coupes have already been sold; subsequent limited runs of up to 60 cars will have a sticker price about 20 percent higher.

Beneath the skin is a stock Viper frame to which an FIA-spec cage has been added. There is a large X-shape crossmember that fits over the engine and a full cage in the cockpit. This additional bracing has increased torsional stiffness by 200 percent.

The engine modifications are minimal. There's a new cam, a reduced backpressure exhaust system with no catalytic converters, and a modified oil pan to increase oil pressure (the system remains a wet sump).

On paper, the engine produces 520 brake horsepower and 540 lb-ft of torque, although [Tommy] Archer hints that the horsepower is probably closer to the torque number. The transmission is fitted with a larger cooler and has a shorter-throw linkage. The engine has a lighter flywheel, and the stock electronically controlled limited-slip differential has been replaced by the viscous-coupled racing diff from the GTS/R.

After crawling through the cage and settling down into the seat, I pull on my helmet and get strapped in. A flip on the toggle switch for the electrical system energizes the car and a push of the stock engine-start button brings the Competition Coupe to life with a bark.

The Tremec 6-speed snaps sharply into first and the clutch takeup feels almost as light as the production car's. I push hard on the throttle, and the car responds instantly. In testing, Hong is able to wring out a 3.7-sec. 0–60 time and an 11.7-sec. quarter mile at 122.9 miles per hour. This tremendous grip is reflected in the 1.15g Hong records on the skidpad and the fastest recorded slalom speed in *Road & Track* testing: 78.3 miles per hour. The Competition Coupe is still no match for the purpose-built GTS/R, which cost three times as much, [but] is the closest thing to buying a turn-key mid-pack Trans-Am car directly from a manufacturer.

~Road & Track, April 2003

The stock SRT-10 is a good track car and a vast improvement over the original Viper, so the Competition Coupe looked deeply promising on paper. It proves itself on the tight Firebird track chosen for our encounter. In a straight line, the coupe gobbles up the blacktop, and there's more than enough torque to light up the rear slicks. Dodge claims the car will sprint to 60 miles per hour in 3.7 seconds, with 100 miles per hour arriving 5.5 seconds later—very swift indeed. With straight pipes emerging alongside your eardrums, there's a hard-edged V-10 bark that is muffled away on the street car.

Aside from the need to exercise care when squeezing the engine's trigger, this is a friendly car. The brakes are phenomenal, grip is stellar (we saw 1.5g lateral on the telemetry traces), and the handling is sweet. You expect a big car to understeer and feel a little clumsy, but the Competition Coupe just noses into apexes and shrinks with familiarity. Start throwing it around, and the chassis talks back to you, its messages coming through loud and clear. The car feels like a serious racing machine tuned by serious racing people.

~Automobile Magazine, April 2003

Built on a (highly) modified SRT-10 chassis.

Competition Coupes are built for track use only and do not come with a VIN.

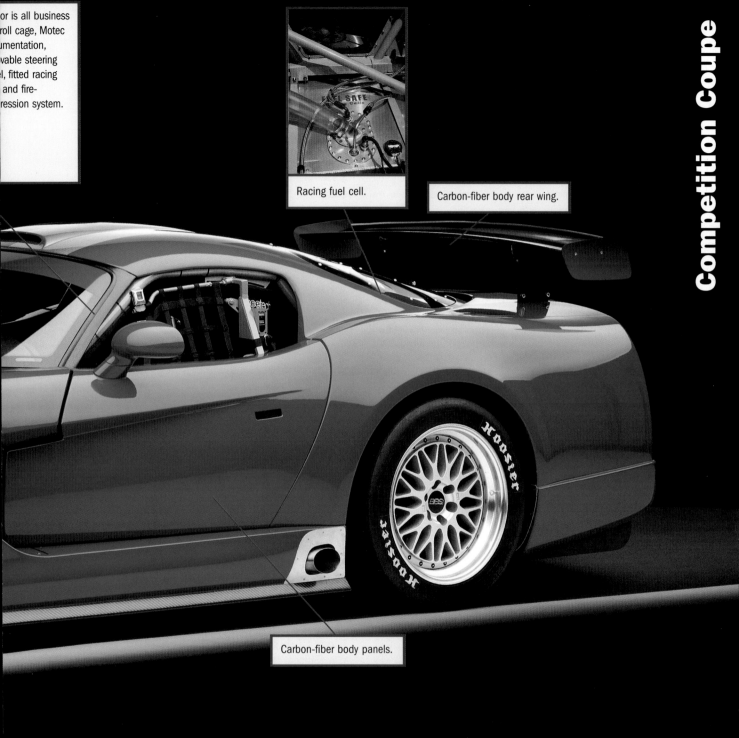

...or is all business
...roll cage, Motec
...umentation,
...vable steering
...el, fitted racing
... and fire-
...ression system.

Racing fuel cell.

Carbon-fiber body rear wing.

Carbon-fiber body panels.

Ron Kimball

Chapter 7

Special Vipers

Through Viper history, the factory has produced a few one-off cars. While not likely to be trading hands very often, it's worth documenting them for future reference.

1996 White GTS Coupes
All production 1996 GTS coupes were blue with white stripes—except three, which were painted the reverse white with blue stripes (not to be confused with the later GT2 cars). These three special coupes were built for Chrysler execs Tom Gale, Francois Castaing, and Team Viper Interior Manager Sandy Emerling.

Also, two blue with white stripes coupes left the factory with white five-spoke wheels instead of the usual polished finish. One went to then VCA National Secretary Jon Brobst, the other to VCA's Los Angeles Region President Drew Alcazar.

Three 1996 coupes were built in white with blue stripes for Chrysler execs. This car was awaiting matching wheels and a gas cap, which were in short supply at the beginning of production. Owner: Tom Gale.

1997 All-blue RT/10
One 1997 RT/10 was built in solid blue (without the white stripes) with a solid black interior (without the body-color-accented interior trim pieces).

VCA First National Secretary, Jon Brobst, was the first factory pick-up and took his blue GTS with white wheels home behind his matching blue with white stripes Indy Dodge Ram. Owner: Jon Brobst.

1998 "Smoothie Hood" RT/10
In 1998, the RT/10 received the GTS's hood with the NACA duct and air vents over the wheels. One RT/10 (VIN 1B3ER65E*WV400408) was shipped with a smooth hood and pre-1998 front fascia.

Viper Club of America Raffle Cars
VCA National President and co-founder Steve Ferguson convinced Dodge to build a one-off Viper each year for the Viper Club of America to raffle off and generate funds through the sales of tickets. Viper Club of America members could purchase tickets at $100 a piece (typically between 1,000 and 2,000 tickets were sold).

The first VCA raffle car, was the this three-tone GTS ACR. Owner: Mitch Wehrly

One of the prettiest VCA raffle cars is this one-off blue with silver stripes GTS/ACR. Owner: Wayne Finch.

All ACRs were GTS coupes, except this one RT/10 built as a raffle car for the VCA.

2000 Black, Silver, and Gray GTS ACR

For the sixth Viper Owner's Invitational (VOI) held in St. Louis, Dodge created this special three-tone GTS ACR as the raffle car, using the three colors then available on the Viper: black, steel gray, and silver. The GTS had red VOI 6 "Rollin' On the River" graphics as well.

2001 Graphite RT/10 ACR

This 2001 RT/10 was painted the next year's 2002 color of metallic graphite. But what makes this RT/10 even more special is that it is the only RT/10 ever built with the ACR package (performance shocks, BBS wheels, harnesses, and K&N air filters with smooth tubes). The raffle car came with a cognac interior and black powder-coated BBS wheels.

This wild paint job represents the country music theme of the 7th Viper Owner's Invitational held in Nashville, TN. The neck of the guitar runs down the side of the car and the strings run over the hood. Owner: George Nunes.

The first production yellow with black stripes SRT-10 was built as a VCA raffle car. Owner: Trinh Thai.

Fifty blue with white strips 2004 Ram SRT.10s were built for VCA members to purchase; One was raffled off. Owner: Nabil Arafat

This was the crime-fighting version of the Viper in the TV show *Viper*.

2002 Blue with Silver Stripes GTS ACR

To commemorate the end of production for the GTS, Dodge built this special GTS/ACR in the original 1996 blue color, but this time with silver stripes, which looked especially good with the ACR's silver BBS wheels.

2003 Nashville SRT-10

The 2003 raffle car was the new 2003 SRT-10. The paint scheme was done in red, purple, orange, gold, and maroon. The design reflected the Nashville theme of VOI 7, with the body of a guitar along the side of the car and the neck and strings stretching over the hood with the snake emblem.

2004 Yellow with Black Stripes SRT-10

The 2004 raffle car was the first production Viper SRT-10 built in yellow. It also featured dual tapering black stripes, similar to those seen on the GTS/R concept car.

2004 Blue with White Stripes Ram SRT-10

To commemorate the new Viper-powered truck, Dodge built 50 of the Ram SRT-10s in blue with white stripes for purchase by Viper Club of America members only. One truck was raffled off and won by VCA Ontario President, Nabil Arafat. The truck features special Viper club floor mats and logos, as well as a plaque autographed by Wolfgang Bernhard, chief operations officer of DaimlerChrysler and honorary Chairman of the Viper Club of America.

Non-Production Cars

Defender

The Viper had its own crime-fighting TV show for three seasons. When a button was pushed on the stock-looking Viper, it would morph into the silver "Defender." Because Defenders were built on pre-production Viper chassis, Chrysler requested that they

The 2000 Viper GTS/R concept led the styling direction for the SRT-10 and Competition Coupe.

The Viper SRT-10 concept car had slightly less rise in the fenders than the production version.

The original RT/10 concept car now resides at the Walter P. Chrysler Museum in Auburn Hills, MI.

Viper GTS concept car featured an LED strip across the spoiler instead of the production snake emblem.

all be destroyed when the series was cancelled, so the parts would not end up in consumer hands.

Concept Cars

The key Viper concept cars (all are still in DaimlerChrysler's possession) are the original Viper RT/10 roadster, the blue with white stripes GTS coupe, the 2000 red with silver stripes GTS/R concept coupe (which set the look for the SRT-10 convertible),

John Hennessey's Viper Venom 650R does 0–60 miles per hour in 3.0 seconds, making it the quickest car on street tires *Motor Trend* has ever tested.

and the SRT-10 convertible concept car (which has slightly less dramatic fenders than the production version).

Tuner Cars

Modifications rarely add to the value of a car, as the majority of buyers prefer an all original car, even if they plan to modify it themselves. Indeed, in some cases, modifications can detract from the value of a car. Two tuner cars worth mentioning because they are likely to be advertised as such: Fitzgerald Dodge's Shelby Vipers and Hennessey Motorsports' Venom Vipers.

In 1995, Fitzgerald Dodge teamed with Carroll Shelby to sell a limited-edition Shelby Viper. The first one, called the Shelby Viper RT/10 CS, was based on an RT/10. The Vipers were repainted Wimbledon White with blue stripes and featured several Shelby logos all over the vehicle. The cross hair in the grill was removed, leaving a gaping-mouth opening similar to the original Cobra. Fitzgerald planned to produce 50 of these cars, but in the end, only 22 were produced. The cars were not numbered sequentially, so it is possible to have a dash plaque number higher than 22.

In 1997, a second series was planned based upon the GTS coupe and called the Carroll Shelby Street Competition Viper Coupe. Again, the front fascia was revised to remove the cross-hairs. The coupe was painted red with gold stripes and gold wheels, and had a red interior. Price was $89,900. Fitzgerald planned to build 25 of these Vipers, but only one was produced.

What They Said in 1993: 1993 Hennessey 550

If fast, exclusive, expensive cars are fun—which they are, or why would anyone bother?—then making them faster, more exclusive, and more expensive must make them even more fun, right?

In our testing, the upgrades shaved a half-second from the Viper's already impressive 0-to-60 miles per hour time (from 4.4 seconds to 3.9) and trimmed almost three seconds to 130 miles per hour (from 19.6 to 16.8). Hennessey's plan for the Viper was to give the V-10 roadster a little more power and a much more forceful presence.

Once Hennessey had uncorked the 8.0 liter V-10, it made sense to look around for other incremental gains in airflow. Lower-restriction air-filter elements and ducts . . . enlarged throttle bodies . . . and a ported and polished intake manifold. Intake and exhaust ports . . . are flow-tested, relieved, and polished, and the heads are milled to bump compression from 9.1:1 to an even 10:1. Roller rocker arms giving a little extra leverage open the valves a bit farther while reducing friction. Hennessey . . . installed an eighteen-percent shorter gearset (3.73:1 versus 3.07:1) in the car we tested.

Response, smoothness, flexibility, and drivability were essentially indistinguishable from a stock Viper's. Once the pedal is well and truly down, the Hennessey Viper Venom tears up through the gears with measurably more gusto than a stocker. Quarter-mile performance perks up from 13.1 seconds at 108 miles per hour to 12.7 at 116. The top-speed figure increases from 163 to 170.

~*Car and Driver*, September 1993

What They Said in 2003: Viper SRT-10 Venom 650R

With only 500 horsepower and 525 lb-ft of torque on tap, a stock 2003 Dodge Viper SRT-10 just isn't fast enough for some people. Two years ago, some customers raised concerns about Hennessey's business practices (we heard from a few), and the jury is still out on the validity of those claims. But the distractions haven't stopped Hennessey from developing . . . the Venom 600 and Venom 650R, one of which notched the quickest quarter-mile time we've recorded on stock tires.

Consider that the Venom 650R package includes all the (Venom 600) hardware and takes it to the next level by way of a stroker short-block: The 522-cube 650R incorporates JE 10.8:1 forged pistons, moly rings, longer than stock Manley Pro forged-steel connecting rods, and a custom-machined stroker crankshaft. A Comp Cams roller cam is employed along with an upgraded fuel system and specific computer programming to deliver a wider powerband with gobs more torque than stock.

Independent chassis dyno testing of the Venom 650R verified 587 horsepower and 584 lb-ft of torque measured at the rear tires. That translates to about 690 horses at the flywheel, assuming an industry-standard 15-percent drivetrain loss.

On the highway, the Venom 650R remains docile during cruising—actually even mellower than a stock SRT-10; but at the track, the package is vicious. Running on stock Michelin run-flat 19-inch radials, we drove the Venom 650R to an amazing 10.76-second quarter mile—making this the quickest stock-tired vehicle we've ever tested. We hustled the 650R to a 3.0-second 0-to-60-miles per hour sprint that beats all-wheel-drive super-exotics like the Lamborghini Murcielago by over half a second.

~*Motor Trend*, December 2003

Texan John Hennessey has been modifying Vipers since their inception, beginning with the RT/10. Hennessey has offered the Venom 500, 550, 600, and 650R (representing the approximate horsepower of the packages). While other tuners offer performance parts, Hennessey has perhaps done the best job of marketing a turn-key package.

A company called Autoform in Michigan built a limited number of GTS/R replicas for street use to commemorate the Daytona wins. Painted red with white stripes, the cars were based on a stock 2002 GTS, but wheels, a wing, and other items were added to make it look just like the real race car.

Autoform's GTS Daytona #91 street replica of the winning ORECA car. Owner: Jose Picazo.

Autoform's GTS Daytona replica features a wing similar to the ORECA race cars. Owner: Jose Picazo.

If you pack light, Vipers can be used for some fun road trips! *Maurice Q. Liang*

Chapter 8

Owning a Viper

Owning a Viper

Owning a Viper is not like owning other sports/exotic cars such as Corvettes or Porsches, which are more useable on a daily basis. Vipers have a lot of idiosyncrasies that you have to put up with. Like gas gauges that aren't very accurate, air conditioning that has no temperature adjustment (at least in the first- and second-generation cars), hot side sills that can burn your legs when getting in and out, pedals that are offset to the left, and a desire to rub its chin on any bump higher than a matchbook.

Then of course, there's the attention. You have to get used to coming back to your car and finding fingerprints on it (I once found lip prints on mine!), people driving in your blind spot while they're checking out the car, and everyone wanting rides.

The flip side is, you'll laugh with giddiness every time you stomp on the gas pedal and it catapults you forward with all that massive torque. You'll be amazed at how it seems to defy the laws of physics as it sticks around corners.

Road trips are both a thrill and a challenge. One of the best memories of my life is a three-week road trip I took in my Viper roadster. It wasn't just a trip. It was an adventure. The people I met, the situations I found myself in. It would never happen while driving a Camry. The challenge is packing a trunk that loses half its capacity when you store the roof and side curtains. You learn to pack the car, not your luggage. And you learn to travel light. While it's tempting to remove the spare tire to gain a little more space, Viper engineers don't recommend it. The spare tire is designed in as part of the crush zone, so removing it changes the protection you receive in a rear-end collision.

Maintenance

Fortunately, unlike some exotic cars that require $5,000-plus tune-ups every 15,000 or 30,000 miles, the Viper is relatively low maintenance. Over the past 10 years, the only major expenses my RT/10—with 50,000 miles on it—has incured are:

a new set of tires (you get about 25,000 miles on a set of performance tires like the Michelin Pilots ($970), a replacement for a stone-cracked windshield ($400), new plugs and wires ($150), a new entry receiver module ($81), a new battery ($100), and new thermostat gaskets ($350). The only other expense is oil and filter changes every 3,000 to 5,000 miles—though an oil change does require *10* quarts of Mobil One.

For service, it's best to take your Viper to a Dodge dealer that specializes in servicing Vipers. Check with local Viper Club of America presidents for recommendations. They may also know of independents in your area that specialize in servicing Vipers.

For examples of replacement parts costs, see Appendix IV.

Tips

Take a performance driving school: Yeah, we've all heard it, "I've been driving fast all my life. I know how to drive a performance car!" Put your ego back in your pocket and take a high-performance driving school, preferably one that's familiar with Vipers. Not only will improving *your* skill make your Viper go faster, it might save you, your passenger, and your Viper's life someday.

Resetting the alarm: If the battery runs low (typically when the car hasn't been driven in awhile), the alarm will arm and lock the doors and set the fuel cutoff, making it impossible to start the car. If after the car's battery is replaced or recharged the car does not respond to the key fob, press and hold both the lock and unlock buttons on the key fob for about five seconds to resynchronize the alarm module with the key fob transmitter (on Gen II cars).

Keep the battery charged: The Viper's alarm and electronic memory circuits still put a small drain on the battery, even if the car is not driven. If you don't plan on driving your Viper for awhile

If you're creative, you can fit a lot into a Viper. Travel light and pack the car, rather than your luggage, using every nook and cranny.

(like during the winter months), keep a battery tender (trickle charger) on it to keep the battery from losing its charge.

Hard starting: If your 1996 and later Viper is hard to start—that is, it cranks but won't catch, try cycling the ignition key on and off, leaving it in the on position for a few seconds to cycle the fuel pump. Repeat this about three times, and then try cranking it. If it starts, chances are you need a new fuel pressure relief valve.

Closing the hood: When closing the hood on a Gen I and Gen II Viper, first be sure the guides on the rear of the hood

The Viper Club of America's trunk mat gives the RT/10 trunk a more finished look while protecting your belongings from damage.

are all the way in the tracks. Then, close the hood by pushing down above the springs (about 18 to 24 inches from the front lip of the hood). Do not push the hood down at the front lip.

Protect the spoiler: Nothing makes you cringe like the sound of the front spoiler scrape against the pavement or curb. The nose of the Viper is very low and is farther out there than appears from the driver's seat. When approaching a parking curb, stay further back than you think you should. Don't wait until you feel contact. It's too late. Approach speed bumps, drains, and driveways at a 45-degree angle if possible, so the tires contact the rise before the bodywork.

Downshifting into third gear: Your arm's natural tendency when down-shifting from fourth into third gear is to push forward and slightly to the right. But with the Viper's six-speed, you'll likely bump into the shift gate. If you experience this problem, try pushing straight forward.

Go easy on the gas at first: When you first get your Viper, it's tempting to just blast from stop light to stop light. But the most common cause of Viper accidents is the back end coming around due to the driver getting on the gas too hard

or too abruptly, especially in mid-corner. The huge amount of torque breaks the rear tires free, causing them—and the car—to spin. So, before jumping on the throttle, make sure your Viper is aimed straight, and ease into the throttle when exiting a corner.

Drive the car! It's amazing how many Vipers have fewer than 5,000 miles on them, even after 10 years. This is a driver's car—maybe the ultimate driver's car—yet you'll never be comfortable with driving it unless you drive it a lot. Practice makes perfect, as they say. Besides, driving the Viper is more than half the fun of owning it. It's not fragile, so get out there and drive it!

Accesories

Basic accessories you should consider purchasing if your car doesn't come with them are:

Floor mats and trunk mats protect your carpet. The Viper club's mats won't bunch up or slip around like the factory mats—to order, go to: http://norcal.viperclub.org.

Car cover: Buy a lightweight cotton or polycotton (but not nylon) cover for traveling. They take up less space than the Evolution fabric covers.

California Duster: to dust the car off without scratching it after each drive.

EBC "Green" brake pads: for less brake dust than stock pads.

Radar detector: A good one. Like the Valentine One.

A bra: If the nose of your Viper is still relatively free of stone chips and scrapes, protect it with a bra. Speed Lingerie makes a nice, color-coordinated bra (They even have them with stripes!) or you can have the clear plastic film applied to the nose. Fastrack makes a three-prong metal guard that bolts under the spoiler to protect the bottom of the spoiler from scrapes against curbs.

Other popular exterior accessories include hardtops, side windows, rear wings, wheels and tires, front and rear fascias, front and side wind splitters, hood louvers, custom hoods, and custom paint.

Inside, accessories include custom upholstery, racing seats, racing harnesses, and custom dashboards and trim.

Visit www.viperclub.org and www.viperbuyersguide.com for current listings of Viper accessories suppliers.

Hardtops, Side Windows, Tonneau Covers

The factory hardtop features a double bubble design.

Two of the most popular accessories for RT/10s are hardtops and side windows. *Jay Herbert gives a rundown on the more popular ones that have been available.*

Adding a hardtop to a Viper RT/10 will do many things. Visually, it will make the car look longer and lower. Inside, it will be quieter. Typically, the side windows seal better against the hardtop, and combined with the headliner, significantly reduces noise inside the car. The downside of a hardtop is you can't just toss it in the trunk when the sun comes out, since it doesn't fit.

Hardtop manufacturers include Mopar, Northwind Engineering, Autoform, V-Mania, TGF, and Rawlson.

There are several things to consider when choosing a hardtop. For example, some tops just drop right on (Northwind, V-Mania, and later Mopar tops) using stock Viper hardware and mounting points, while others (Autoform and Rawlson) require special hardware to be mounted on your car before the top can be installed. The earlier (pre-1997) Mopar tops require you to remove the pad from the sport bar before installation.

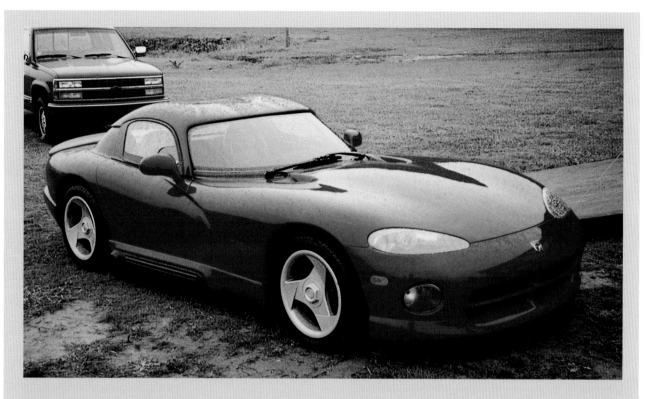

Autoform's top covers the A-pillars to give more of a coupe-like appearance.

Most aftermarket tops have plenty of headroom, but if you plan on taking your Viper on the track, you should be sure there will be enough clearance for your helmet. Lastly, decide if you want to use your stock (or compatible aftermarket) side windows. The design of some aftermarket tops requires the use of matching side curtains. Prices for aftermarket tops typically range from $2,500 to over $7,000.

It's important to note the model year of your Viper and the type of windshield mounting points on your car, particularly if you're purchasing a used top. The pins for the windshield mount on RT/10s changed several times from 1992 to 1996. (Replacement pins are available from Northwind Engineering and Partsrack.) Beginning in 1997, when power side windows were introduced, Vipers used a completely new windshield surround so 1997 and later tops will not work with pre-1997 cars.

Mopar: The Mopar top is the official "factory" top, made by ASC, and available through Dodge dealers. It's a "double-bubble"

design (similar to the coupe's look) and billed as a seasonal top because it requires you to remove the pad on the sport bar before installation. Ninety-seven and later versions do not require the removal of this pad, and there is a netted pocket in the roof for storing sunglasses. These tops are plentiful and many are available used. If you do purchase one used, make sure the top has the correct hardware (front pin length) for your year Viper.

Northwind Engineering: This top is smooth and made out of carbon fiber. It's the lightest of the group and installs just like the factory soft top. The stock side windows work with the Northwind top. Northwind also offers polycarbonate sliding side windows that improve side vision. (You can see the passenger side mirror!) These windows lock and are manufactured with a stout black metal frame. They will also work with the stock soft and hardtops.

Autoform and Rawlson: These tops are both double-bubble designs. They use a cover over the stock Viper windshield

A-pillar, which can be painted body-color to give the RT/10 a more coupe-like appearance. Because of their shape, these tops take a little more room to store and owners must take care to avoid damaging the A-pillar covers. The tops are considered "seasonal" due to the more difficult installation process. Both tops require matching side windows. Autoform's side windows are made of polycarbonate, and, like the Autoform top itself, are still available.

Rawlson's top was distributed in the United States by Hennessey Motorsports, but is no longer produced. Rawlson's side windows were made of glass and deserve a word of caution: the glass side curtains are more difficult to install, heavier, and break into thousands of pieces if accidentally dropped. Getting a replacement for the glass side curtains can be expensive, time-consuming, and maybe even impossible since they are no longer manufactured.

TGF: Made by a division of Metalcrafters, the people who built the original Viper concept car, the TGF top was unique because it sat flush with the sport bar to give the Viper a sleeker look. Of course, headroom suffered a bit, and factory side curtains couldn't be used. The TGF top is no longer available.

V-Mania: V-Mania designed a new double-bubble top for the 1997 and newer RT/10s. Their top has an optional "GTS/R-style" (non-functional) scoop for a more racy look. V-Mania has a unique hardtop in their lineup, a tinted see-through top. V-Mania also offers polycarbonate sliding side windows that will work with the factory tops as well. In addition, V-Mania offers a hardtop for the SRT-10.

ART: Applied Racing Technologies Group of Mansfield, Texas offers a low-profile (flat) carbon fiber hardtop that weighs only 15 pounds.

There are several methods to store hardtops. Autoform and Mopar both sell nice padded tubular top holders. The Mopar holder also has spaces for side curtains/windows. Another method of storing the hardtop is a pulley system, which lifts your roof up off car and hangs it from the garage ceiling. These systems are available in the aftermarket for Miata and Mercedes tops, or if you're handy, for a minimal cost, you can assemble a series of pulleys and hooks that will work just fine.

Driving Schools

Before you add any performance upgrades for your car, upgrade your own performance. Many times I've seen inexperienced Viper drivers bring their highly modified Vipers to the track, only to be left in the dust by a skilled driver driving a stock Viper.

High limits and massive torque can get a driver into trouble in the blink of an eye. No matter how experienced you are, it's wise to attend a performance driving school like Skip Barber Driving School (www.skipbarber.com). Skip Barber uses Dodge Vipers in their school, so you get to drive their Vipers, and their instructors are familiar with the handling characteristics of the Viper—a big difference from an instructor who is used to driving, say, BMWs. Skip Thomas' Viper Days (see www.viperdays.com) is another school where you can drive your *own* Viper on the track. It, too, is tailored specifically to Viper owners.

Performance Upgrades

The simplest way to increase horsepower a bit (10 horsepower, which isn't much when we're talking 450) on Gen I and Gen II cars is to put low-restriction K&N air filters and Mopar's "smooth tubes" air intakes. GT2s and ACRs already come with this.

Many Viper owners also like to change the exhaust to give the car a more aggressive sound. (Drive-by noise regulations prevent Dodge from making the Viper any louder than it is.) The easiest way is to install a new exhaust system from the catalytic converter back (known as a cat-back system). The sound will be louder, the tone will be different, and it's emissions-legal. But don't expect much power increase. To increase horsepower, you need to open up airflow in the intake and all the way through the exhaust system.

Beyond that, increasing horsepower will require internal engine modifications. Some owners and tuners have experimented with superchargers and turbochargers on Vipers with varying degrees of success. But, there is no free lunch. To get this increase in power, you will sacrifice durability and longevity.

Another minor improvement is to add a short-shift kit, which reduces the length of the shifter's throw. A simpler alternative is to install a shorter shift knob, which creates a similar effect.

The Skip Barber Performance Driving School lets you train in their Vipers. *Maurice Q. Liang*

Be aware that in either case, the shift effort increases due to the change in leverage.

If you plan to take your first- or second-generation Viper to the track, you should upgrade the brakes. Use race-compound pads (only at the track), install cooling ducts, and replace the fluid with Motul 600 brake fluid. If you plan to visit the track more than once, it's best to buy a separate set of wheels and mount track tires (either slicks or semi-slicks). That way, if you lock up the brakes at the track, you won't flat spot your expensive street tires. And no, it's not worth trying to save money by driving on semi-slick tires on the street the rest of the time. The sticky tires will just kick up rocks and damage your paint. Used Viper wheels are available for a reasonable price on the Internet and through Viper parts dealers.

You may also wish to install a fire extinguisher and five-point harnesses. All Vipers have the mounting points for five-point harnesses. (ACRs and GT2s came with the harnesses installed.) If you wish to install them, it's best to purchase an extra rear bulkhead cover and cut the slots in it rather than damage your original cover.

For the latest listing of Viper tuners and suppliers, visit www.viperclub.org and www.viperbuyersguide.com.

The Viper Club of America

Even if you're not a club-type person, it's worth joining the Viper Club of America (VCA) just for the information. VCA is the only official Viper owners' club and is recognized and supported by DaimlerChrysler. You'll receive a quarterly magazine called *Viper Magazine*, a membership badge, lia-

Join the Viper club and learn more about Vipers while sharing your passion with fellow enthusiasts. The national club has local regions, such as the Northern California Region shown in this photo. *Ron Kimball*

Nothing can describe the thrill of joining some 800 other Vipers at a Viper Owner's Invitation. *Maurice Q. Liang*

bility insurance coverage at events, access to restricted areas on the Viper club website, discounts on merchandise, special access to Dodge and club events, and membership in a local region. The local regions provide social, track, and technical events, and many publish a regional newsletter as well. To join, fill out the form on the website at www.viperclub.org or call 800-998-1110.

If you participate, you'll find a fun group of enthusiasts who share your passion for this wonderful car. And there's nothing like driving your Viper down the road with a group of other Vipers.

Viper Owners' Invitationals

About every other year, Dodge hosts an international get-together for Viper owners called the Viper Owners' Invitational. It's basically a four-day lovefest for Viper owners. It's held in a different part of the United States every time. Owners come together for parties, autocrossing, open track driving, drag racing, and touring events. It's also a chance to meet the factory people, from the engineers up to the executives. It's an event no Viper owner should miss.

If you follow these tips, you'll be on your way to one of the most exciting experiences of your life. Viper—it's not just a car, it's an experience.

Appendix I

Quick Reference Guide to Major Model Year Changes

RT/10

1992 RT/10
First year of production, 285 cars
Exterior colors: Red
Interior colors: Gray
Engine: 400-horsepower, 465 ft-lb torque, 8.0-liter, V-10
Transmission: Six-speed Borg Warner T-56 manual
Wheels: Directional, silver-painted, Three-spoke cast aluminum
Tires: Michelin XGT 275/40 ZR 17 and 335/35 ZR 17
Side-exit exhaust
No roll-up windows, no external door handles, rudimentary soft top
Antenna on driver's side rear fender
Notch in fender next to fuel door
No reverse lock-out
Brake calipers say "Viper"
Battery located between frame rails under trunk floor
Dual cooling fans
Dealer-installed A/C
Four-rib intake manifold
Leather valise for owner and service manuals

1993 RT/10 (after ~ VIN 605, earlier cars are same as 1992s)
Exterior colors: Red, black
Interior colors: Gray
Windshield antenna
Notch moved to fuel door instead of fender
Reverse lock-out added
Calipers changed to read "RT/10"
Battery moved to outside left frame rail
Single cooling fan
Small leather pouch for owner's manual
Yellow caution zone added to temperature gauge

1994 RT/10
Exterior colors: Red, black, emerald green, yellow
Interior colors: Gray or optional tan
Wheels painted a brighter silver
Yellow caution zone removed from temperature gauge
Factory-installed A/C available
Three-rib intake manifold
Calipers go back to "Viper" around late 1994/early 1995
Fuel filler rubber protector added

GTS

RT/10   GTS

1995 RT/10

Exterior colors: Red, black, emerald green, yellow

Interior colors: Gray or optional tan

New inside passenger door grab handle added

New mesh pockets added to front of seat

Factory double-bubble hardtop available

Underhood insulation pad added

Last 300 sidepipe cars marked with pin-stamping on toe-box (heater cover) under the hood.

1996 RT/10

Exterior colors: White with blue stripes, black with silver stripes, red with yellow wheels

Interior colors: Black (with body-colored steering wheel, shifter knob, and e-brake handle)

New wheels: Five-spoke, painted cast-aluminum

Rear-exit exhaust

New GTS suspension (cast-aluminum A-arms)

Smaller 19-gallon gas tank

Trunk with spare tire cutout

Upgraded cooling system

Tires: Michelin Pilot MXX3 SX: 275/40 ZR 17 and 335/35 ZR 17

Sliding side curtains

New SMC hood replaces RTM hood

Retains older V-10 but with 415 horsepower, 488 ft-lb torque

1996 GTS

New coupe model

Exterior color: Blue with white stripes

Interior color: Black

Wheels: Five-spoke, polished cast- aluminum

New engine: Redesigned 450-horsepower, 490 lb-ft, 8.0-liter, V-10

New tires: Michelin Pilot MXX3 SX 275/40 ZR 17 and 335/35 ZR 17

New seats with perforated leather

New instrument panel

New in-dash CD player by Alpine

In-board seatbelts

Manually adjustable pedal cluster

Dual air bags

Power windows

Stripes go through rear license plate opening

1997 RT/10

Exterior colors: Blue w/white stripes, solid red

Interior colors: Black (w/ body-color steering wheel, shift knob, and e-brake handle). Tan with gold package only.

New engine: 450-horsepower, 490 ft-lb, 8.0-liter V-10

Wheels: Five-spoke polished forged aluminum (optional gold or yellow on red cars)

New interior

Dual air bags

New exterior door handles

New manually adjustable pedal cluster

In-board seatbelts

New power windows

1997 GTS

Exterior colors: Blue w/white stripes or solid red

Interior color: Black only

New wheels: Five-spoke, polished forged aluminum (optional gold or yellow for red cars)

Narrower stripes (don't pass through license plate opening)

1998 RT/10

Exterior colors: Red or silver

Interior color: Black

New hood from GTS w/NACA ducts and vents

New GTS front fascia

New lower-force airbags with cut-off switch

New tubular exhaust

1998 GTS

Exterior colors: Red, red w/silver stripes, silver, or silver w/blue stripes

Interior color: Black

New lower-force air bags with cut-off switch

New tubular exhaust

1998 GT2

100 produced

Exterior color: White w/blue stripes

Interior color: Black w/blue accents

Engine: 460-horsepower, 500 lb-ft, 8.0-liter V-10

Wheels: 18-inch BBS

Tires: Michelin Pilot SX 275/35 ZR 18, 335/30 ZR 18

Rear wing, front splitters, side sills

K&N air filters, smooth tubes

RT/10

1999 RT/10
Exterior colors: Red, black, or silver
Interior colors: Black or optional Cognac
Wheels: 18-inch-wide five-spoke polished
Tires: Michelin Pilot Sports 275/35 ZR 18 and 335/30 ZR 18
Power mirrors
Cloth sun visors
Satin aluminum interior trim
Golf ball shift knob
No fog lamp covers

2000 RT/10
Exterior colors: Red, black, or steel gray
Interior colors: Black or optional Cognac
Revised engine package

2001 RT/10
Exterior colors: Red, sapphire blue, or Viper Race Yellow
Interior colors: Black or Cognac
New ABS brakes

2002 RT/10
Exterior colors: Red, Viper Race Yellow, or graphite metallic
Interior colors: Black or Cognac

2003 SRT-10
All new design
Exterior colors: Red, black, and silver.
Interior color: Black
Engine: 500-horsepower, 525 lb-ft, 8.3-liter V-10
Transmission: Six-speed Tremec manual
Wheels: 10x18 inches front, 13x19 inches rear
Tires: Michelin ZP1 run-flats, 275/35 ZR 18 and 345/30 ZR 19
Manual folding top
Sidepipes
Power adjustable pedals
14-inch disk brakes

2004 SRT-10
Exterior colors: Red, black, silver, 200 Mamba editions in white
Interior color: Black. All white cars came with two-tone red and black
    "Mamba" interior
Red brake calipers
Late intro convertible boot cover
New trunk carpet kit

GTS

1999 GTS
Exterior colors: Red, red w/silver stripes, black, black w/silver stripes,
    silver, or silver w/blue stripes
Interior colors: Black or optional Cognac
Wheels: 18-inch-wide five-spoke polished
Tires: Michelin Pilot Sports 275/35 ZR 18 and 335/30 ZR 18
Power mirrors
Cloth sun visors
Satin aluminum interior trim
Golf ball shift knob
Remote hatch release
No fog lamp covers
Optional ACR performance package

2000 GTS
Exterior colors: Red, red w/silver stripes, black, black w/silver stripes,
    steel gray, steel gray w/silver stripes
Interior colors: Black or optional Cognac
Revised engine package

2001 GTS
Exterior colors: Red, red w/silver stripes, sapphire, sapphire w/silver
    stripes, yellow, or yellow w/black stripes
Interior colors: Black or Cognac
New ABS brakes

2002 GTS
Exterior colors: Red, red w/silver stripes, yellow, yellow w/black stripes,
    graphite metallic, graphite w/silver stripes
Interior colors: Black or Cognac
Final 360 edition: Red w/white stripes, dash plaque, red stitching

Competition Coupe
Track-only race car
Exterior color: Primer (paint optional)
Engine: 520-horsepower, 540 lb-ft, 8.3-liter V-10
Wheels: Three-piece 18-inch BBS
Tires: Michelin Pilot slicks 305/35 ZR 18 & 345/30 ZR 18
Carbon-fiber body panels
FIA safety cage
Fire-suppression system
Motec instrumentation

Appendix II

Vehicle Identification Numbers (VINs)

Decoding Viper VINs

Every street-legal Viper has a vehicle identification number (VIN). As an example, this VIN is for a 1996 Viper GTS: 1B3ER69E*TV200018. To decode this VIN:

Position	Interpretation	Description
1	Country of Origin	1 = United States
2	Make	B = Dodge
3	Vehicle Type	3 = Passenger Car
4	Passenger Safety	E = Active Driver and Passenger Air Bags
		B = Manual Seatbelts
5	Car Line	R = Viper
6	Series	6 = Performance/Image
7	Body Style	9 = Specialty Coupe (GTS)
		5 = Open Body (roadster)
8	Engine	E = 8.0-liter, 10-cylinder
9	Check Digit	(Used to authenticate valid VIN)
10	Model Year	N=1992, P=1993, R=1994, S=1995, T=1996 etc. (O and Q skipped because they look like zeros)
11	Assembly Plant	V = New Mack or Conner Avenue
12–17	Sequence Number	Number assigned by assembly plant

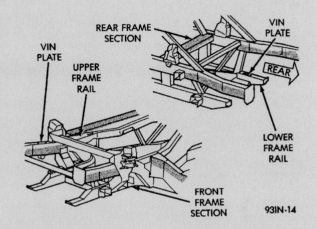

Every vehicle that comes out of an assembly plant is assigned a sequence number, regardless of the make or model. In the Viper's case, from 1992 to 1996, only Vipers were built at the New Mack Plant and (then) Conner Avenue Assembly Plants, so the numbers are sequential and correspond to the number of Vipers built (e.g., if the last VIN sequence was 1166, then 1,166 Vipers were built that year, excluding any pilot or pre-production units).

However, from 1997 to 2002 (excluding 1998, when no Prowlers were built), the Plymouth/Chrysler Prowler was also assembled at the Conner Avenue Assembly Plant, and although the Prowler VIN has different characters for make, car line, etc., the sequence number was continuously assigned regardless of whether it was a Viper or a Prowler. Hence, a Viper built during one of these years could have a VIN sequence number that's higher than the total number of Vipers built that year.

The VIN sequence does *not* necessarily correspond to the order in which the car was built. While collectors frequently like to say something like, "My VIN is 246, so I have the 246th car built," that's not necessarily true. For example, plant documentation shows that in 1996, VIN 18 was actually built before VIN 14–16.

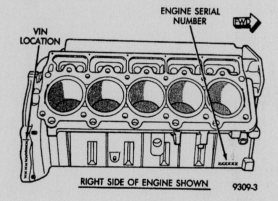

RIGHT SIDE OF ENGINE SHOWN   9309-3

Matching Numbers

The VIN is stamped on a number of places and parts on a car. In addition to the driver's side windshield post, the VIN also appears on the frame, the engine, and the transmission. (See diagrams.) Typically, collectors prefer a car that has all the original parts, so all the VINs stamped on these parts should match, hence the term "numbers-matching car." If a replacement engine is installed, the VIN on the engine will not be the same as the VIN on the chassis, and the car is no longer a "numbers-matching car."

While functionally the car is fine, it may reduce the car's collector value. As mentioned previously, if the Viper has had its engine replaced through factory warranty coverage, be sure to obtain the documentation to prove it.

Body-Code Plate

Unlike most other cars, Vipers offered few factory options. Aside from air conditioning, which became a factory-installable option in 1994, the only other major options were the tan or Cognac interiors, stripes on the GTS, the gold or yellow wheel packages in 1997, and the 1999+ ACR performance package (with the option to add back the deleted luxury equipment) for GTSs. Even the in-trunk CD changer was a dealer-installed accessory.

Because of this limited number of options, the Viper does not come with a body-code plate.

Appendix III

Production Numbers

While there are some holes, the following production data are the most complete available. It is used with permission from the International Viper Registry. All rights reserved.

Viper Production by Model Year

Year	Total Units
1992	285
1993	1,043
1994	3,083
1995	1,577
1996 RT/10	721
1996 GTS	1,166
1997 RT/10	117
1997 GTS	1,671
1998 RT/10	379
1998 GTS	837
1999 GTS (Incl. ACR)	699
1999 ACR	215
2000 RT/10	840
2000 GTS (Incl. ACR)	949
2000 ACR	218
2001 RT/10	874
2001 GTS (Incl. ACR)	877
2001 ACR	227
2002 RT/10	545
2002 GTS (Incl. ACR)	918
2002 ACR	159

Notes:
Total 1997 Viper build: 1,788 (1,762 retail, 26 Pilots)
The 1998 numbers include 12 pilot and pre-production units (6 roadsters and 6 coupes), which will not be sold.

RT/10 Roadster Exterior and Interior Color Production Information

| Year | Exterior | | | | | | | | | Interior | | | Wheels | | | | | |
	Black	Red	Green	Yellow	White	Blue	Silver	Steel Gray	Graphite Metallic	Black	Cognac	Gray	Polished	Gold	Painted	Yellow	GT2	White
1992	1[1]	285	1[1]	1[1]						11		285			285			
1993	115[2]	928[2]																
1994	687[2]	2,189[2]	133[2]	83[2]														
1995	514	458	307	298							572	1,005						
1996	231[2]	166[2]			324[2]					716	2	3						
1997		64				53				114	3		114	3				
1998		252					127						379					
1999	210	128				211				380	169							
2000	259	255						296		306	534		840					
2001		256		356		252		1		656	218		873		1			
2002		181		178					186	459	86		545					

[1] - Exterior color changed (from red), interior changed (from gray) by factory as development/trial
[2] - Estimated

Notes:
1997: Three red 1997 RT/10s were ordered with the "Gold Package" (gold sparkle wheels, and gold snake emblems on the hood's sides) and a tan interior. This is the lowest factory-shipped color combination to date. One solid blue RT/10 (no white stripes) with black steering wheel, shift knob, e-brake manufactured.

1998: Last car off the line was a red roadster on December 11, 1998. One 1998 RT/10 (VIN 1B3ER65E*WV400408) was accidentally shipped with a smooth hood and pre-1998 RT/10 fascia. All other 1998 RT/10s were manufactured with NACA duct and vented hood and GTS style front fascia.

1999: 169 Roadsters with Cognac Connolly Leather interior: 3 Red, 50 Silver, 116 Black.

2000: All RT/10s were built with five-spoke polished wheels.

2001: One Steel Gray ACR RT/10 has a tan interior and black powder-coated ACR-BBS wheels, VIN 1B3ER69E*2V102035, Viper Club of America raffle car.

GTS Coupe Exterior and Interior Color Production Information

Year	Exterior									Interior			Wheels					
	Blue	Red	White	Silver	Steel Gray	Black	Yellow	Sapphire Blue	Graphite Metallic	Black	Cognac	Blue	Polished	Gold	Painted	Yellow	GT2	White
1996	1,163		3							1,166			1,161					5
1997	965	706								1,671			1,657	7[1]		14[2]		
1998		447	102	288						735		102	735				100	
1999		116		250		333				571	128							
2000		166			292	273							731					
2001		144					291	216		575	76		651					
2002		458					120		181	723	36		759					

[1] - Gold wheels and hood side emblem on red coupes, black interior
[2] - Yellow wheels on red coupes

Notes:

1997: Fourteen yellow-wheeled GTSs, and seven gold-wheeled (not "Gold Package," these did not have tan interiors) GTSs manufactured.

1998: 1,076 polished wheels total, 38 painted wheels total, 47 roadsters shipped with factory hardtops, 198 roadsters shipped with optional tonneau covers, all 1998 white cars were GT2 limited edition White with Blue stripes/Blue interior of which two were engineering cars not included in the special 100-car VIN sequence. GT2 cars ran down the line in VIN sequence order (1-100), these are the only Vipers ever to be run in sequence. Last car off the line was a red roadster on 12/11/98. Lowest-build car was a single roadster shipped with a smooth (no NACA or vent ducts) hood and pre-1998 RT/10 front fascia.

1999: 247 of 699 coupes had stripes. 87 of 250 silver w/blue, 30 of 116 red w/silver stripes, 130 of 333 black w/silver stripes; 128 coupes with Cognac Connolly Leather interior: 3 red (late release), 22 silver, 77 black, 26 black with silver stripes.

2000: All non-ACR GTSs (except VCA raffle car) were built with five-spoke polished wheels. * One Factory custom-painted black and silver GTS with harnesses and ACR BBS rims was built as the VCA.

2002: Final edition GTSs were built with an exclusive red/white paint scheme with red stitching on the interior. There were 360 made, with 326 being non-ACR cars.

GTS ACR Coupe Exterior and Interior Color Production Information

Year	Blue	Red	Silver	Exterior Steel Gray	Black	Yellow	Sapphire Blue	Graphite Metallic	Interior Black	Cognac	Wheels BBS
1999		36	81		98						215
2000		60		85	73				218		218
2001		60				89	77		227		227
2002	1	79				40		39	159		159

Notes:

1999: Only 9 ACRs were built without A/C and Stereo Comfort Group.

2000: Only 17 ACRs were built without A/C and Stereo Comfort Group.

2001: Only 4 ACRs were built without A/C and Stereo Comfort Group.

2002: Only 8 ACRs were built without A/C and Stereo Comfort Group. One special Blue/Silver ACR built for Viper Club of America raffle. There were 34 Final Edition GTS ACRs built with an exclusive red/white paint scheme with red stitching on the interior.

Appendix IV

Replacement Parts

If you're contemplating turning that "needs minor repair" wreck into a show-winning Viper, be sure to factor in the time and cost of finding replacement parts. Many of the replacement parts for Vipers are no longer available and those that are, are not always the same as the original parts.

With the limited production volume of Vipers, it's unlikely there'll ever be much of a reproduction parts market, so used parts may be the only way to go. Several dismantlers specialize in Viper parts (see www.viper-buyersguide.com for a current listing). Jon Brobst from Partsrack (360.837.3937 or www.partsrack.com), one of the better-known Viper dismantlers, gives examples on the challenge of finding replacement parts for Vipers:

The Challenge of Finding Replacement Parts

With the low-volume, hand-crafted Viper, and the small-team approach, it was possible for the factory to make ongoing improvements to the Viper in a relatively quick time frame. Consequently, between 1992 and 1993, over 200 running design changes were made, each intended to improve a specific process or component or eliminate a perceived problem. This makes parts-specifying difficult for early cars. While some parts are interchangeable, many are not.

For example, let's say you need a replacement soft top. One top should fit all the roadsters, right? Wrong. Between 1992 and 1996 alone, the front pins that secure the soft top to the windshield header came in three different styles with seven different lengths! Complicating matters further, the top material changed from a pebble-grained vinyl to a cloth-like material in 1993.

Styling changes create their own problems. Even "service parts" (i.e., replacement parts from the dealer) used to fix damaged or worn parts are often unavailable in the factory-original style. When the GTS debuted,

a new front fascia with a more pronounced chin spoiler superseded the original-style fascia. Not only is the style different, but 1992 to 1998 Vipers had the Lexan foglight covers, held in place by three tabs. Since Vipers from 1999 on do not have foglight covers, the newer-style fascias do not have the slots for these covers.

The GTSs and 1996 and later RT/10s also came with a new SMC hood with the NACA duct and louvers, replacing the old "smoothie" hood made from RTM. Dodge no longer stocks (services) the old-style smoothie hood, so rebuilders and restorers must turn to the ever-dwindling supply of used parts from dismantlers. Some owners who plan to keep their Viper forever will buy a spare hood and fascia, just in case.

Front-end crashes usually take out the radiator and fan assembly. Owners of early cars with the twin fan setup will find it nearly impossible to locate new core supports, fans, and radiators. Often, their only choice is to replace them with the current Gen II single fan and newer (or aftermarket) radiators. But one day soon, Gen II parts will likewise be difficult to obtain.

The 3-spoke wheels on 1992–1995 RT/10s are unidirectional, and since the front and rear wheels are different sizes, they are "position specific," i.e., a right rear wheel will only go in the right rear position. It's not uncommon for the right rear wheel to become gouged when bumped against a curb during parallel parking. Dismantlers and used wheel vendors typically sell four to five right-side wheels for every left-side wheel, which results a shorter supply (and higher prices) for the right side wheels. The painted white, yellow, gold, and silver wheels from 1996 and 1997 Vipers are now very rare, or nearly impossible to locate.

Spinouts or crashes that impact the suspension can create a nightmare for Gen I owners. Lower control arms are no longer available from Dodge, causing a dramatic increase in prices for used ones, if they can be found.

Roof pin from a 1993 RT/10.

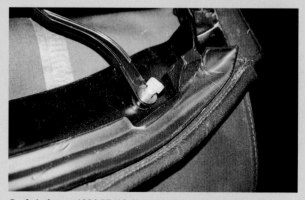

Roof pin from a 1994 RT/10. Note the change in style and length.

The infamous "Green Doohickey." Does your Viper still have one?

The 1992-2000 rear brake calipers are not rebuildable, and are difficult to find and expensive. With the introduction of ABS, Dodge switched to a readily available Ford rear caliper in 2001. Fortunately, the front calipers are rebuildable.

While electrical component failure is rare—even in older Vipers—relay meltdowns or other events that destroy a wiring harness (like a voracious rodent!) can become a nightmare to repair since the original OE wiring harnesses are no longer available.

Replacement interior parts for the optional and limited-production tan and Cognac interiors are in short supply. Other common-wear interior parts such as carpet, seat bolsters, door trim, door-window bezels, sport-bar pads, and the 1992–1996 "fuzzy gray" dashboards are virtually nonexistent. Even the 1996–1997 Gen II flat-black dashes are almost gone.

Perhaps the most interesting hard-to-find part is not even an official part. It's the infamous "Green Doohickey" found under the hood. As the frame was being painted, workers simply installed a small green protective screw cap on the grounding post, used for battery charging and jumpstarting. This cap stopped the protective electrostatic paint from coating this post. Assembly craftsmen at the Viper plant simply left this piece on the post for 6 years of Viper production. It had no part number, no internal cost factor—but every 1992 to 1996 Viper RT/10 had one! However, many dealers and owners discarded the Doohickey when they discovered it had no function. But with no part number, it's impossible to replace.

You can see the importance of retaining your original parts or finding a car that has its original parts. In a few years, when Viper owners hold concours events like many other marques, some gray-haired, anal-retentive perfectionist judge (like me!) will be searching for signs of worn, missing, or replaced items, looking to turn a coveted 100-point Viper into a 99-point car. And the "Green Doohickey" may eventually become the 1-point spoiler of 1992-1996 Vipers!

Typical Replacement Parts Prices (Retail)[2]

These are typical and approximate retail prices for replacement parts. Prices may vary for specific models and years so check with your Dodge dealer for exact prices and availability.

Gen I and II hood	
(unpainted, not including mounting hardware)	$19,000
Gen I and II front fascia (unpainted)	$1,675
Gen I side sills	
(each, unpainted, left and right differ in price)	$2,200--$2,600
Gen II side sills	
(each, unpainted, left and right differ in price)	$4,044-$4,350,
Foglight covers (pair)	$116
1992-2002 headlight assembly (each)	$615
Hood crest	$60
Replacement RT/10 soft top	$3,100
1992-1995 side curtains (including bag)	$835
Side curtain grommets (each)	$48
Rear bulkhead cover	$1065
Sport cap pad	$1035
1992-1995 Steering wheel (pre-air bag)	$750
1996-2002 Steering wheel (w/air bag)	$1,100
1992-1995 RT/10 shift knob (black)	$204
1992-1995 RT/10 driver's seat	$1150
1992-1995 RT/10 dashboard	$372
1996-2002 GTS dashboard	$364
1996-2002 V-10 engine (no longer in stock)	$15,000
1997 polished five-spoke rear wheel	$1,165
1999 wide-five-spoke rear wheel	$1,275
1999-2002 18-inch BBS rear wheel	$3035
275/40 ZR 17 Michelin Pilot Sport (front tire)	$289
335/35 ZR 17 Michelin Pilot Sport (rear tire)	$331
Wiper motor assembly	$484-$500
Heater air vent gasket (only available in a package)	$111

Note, Viper club members often receive discounts on parts from participating dealers. Used parts from Viper dismantlers are often 50% less, so check first. Also, if you're not after original replacement parts, many times aftermarket parts (such as carbon-fiber hoods) are available for much less. Check www.viperclub.org and www.viperbuyersguide.com for current suppliers.

Viper SRT-10 Parts Prices

Here are some example prices for factory replacement parts for the new SRT-10. Prices are retail prices, but check with your dealer for exact prices.

Hood	$3,170
Front fender	$1,160
Front fascia	$995
Hood emblem	$78
Front wheel	$2,875
Rear wheel	$2,875
Side sill	$810
Replacement convertible top	$1,340
Steering wheel	$409
Shift knob	$135
Dash panel	$1,340

[2] Prices provided by Hartzheim Dodge and Partsrack.

Appendix V

Additional Resources

Viper Buyer's Guide Website
The Viper Buyer's Guide website lists updates to this book as well as resources to enhance your Viper experience.
www.viperbuyersguide.com

The Viper Club of America
The official international club for Viper owners with local chapters in the United States, Canada, Europe, and Japan. Dues include a subscription to *Viper Magazine*, liability insurance coverage, membership badge, merchandise discounts, access to Viper club events, subscription to local chapter's newsletter, and access to special programs.

The club's website features classified ads, archives for answers to commonly asked questions, and a wealth of information.
www.viperclub.org
800.998.1110

Viper Magazine
A full-color, quarterly magazine dedicated to Vipers. Features product news, tech tips, club event coverage, as well as listings for Viper parts suppliers. Call 800.998.1110 to subscribe.

Viper
By Matthew Stone
ISBN 0-7603-1767-4
Published by MBI Publishing Company

Covers the development history of the Dodge Viper. Approximately 100 pages with full color photos. Recently updated with additional information and photos.

Dodge Viper Performance Portfolio 1990–1998
Compiled by R. M. Clarke
ISBN 1-85520-472X
Published by Brookland Brooks

Reprints of magazine test reports from *Motor Trend*, *Road & Track*, *Autocar*, *Car and Driver*, and others, covering the Viper RT/10 prototypes through the 1998 GTS and RT/10. 140 pages, black and white.

Road & Track Dodge Viper Portfolio 1992–2002
ISBN 1-85520–6102
Published by Brookland Books and *Road & Track*

Reprints of *Road & Track* test reports covering the Viper from the original concept car article in 1989 to the beginning of the third-generation SRT-10. 136 pages in black and white and color.

Dodge Viper
By Daniel F. Carney
ISBN 0-7603-0984-1
Published by MBI Publishing Company

Covers the development and production of the Viper from concept RT/10 through the Gen III SRT-10. Includes racing versions. 166 pages in full color.

Viper Pure Performance by Dodge
By the Auto Editors of Consumer Guide
ISBN 0-7853-0109-7
Published by Publications International, Ltd.

The first book written about the Viper, covering the development of the RT/10 (only). 80 pages in color.

Index

Dodge Viper
ISBN 0-7603-0984-1

Viper
ISBN 0-7603-1767-4

Snake Bit
ISBN 0-7603-1781-X

Cars of the Gran Turismo
ISBN 0-7603-1495-0

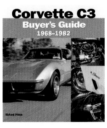

**Corvette C3
Buyer's Guide**
ISBN 0-7603-1655-4

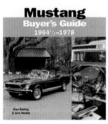

**Mustang
Buyer's Guide**
ISBN 0-7603-1547-7

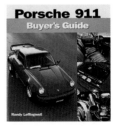

Porsche 911 Buyer's Guide
ISBN 0-7603-0947-7

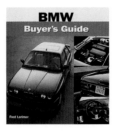

BMW Buyer's Guide
ISBN 0-7603-1099-8

Corvette Buyer's Guide
ISBN 0-7603-1009-2